Gift Aid

20   70897048 5822

On Grief and Bereavement

How to Keep Living After the Loss of a Loved One, Find Meaning & Heal Your Heart

Rob Watts

Table of Contents

Introduction

Like a constellation of stars, we are all slowly revolving around each other, and when one of those stars suddenly vanishes, we spin off course. When a light that had guided us and kept us company is suddenly snuffed out by death, we lose all momentum, and we feel like the universe now makes no sense, and that we no longer belong to it.

This is grief.

It is a fact that we will all eventually die. Death is a part of life, though most of us don't want to talk about it. Instead, we see it as a scary prospect, like a contagious disease that you attract just by mentioning it. This has created societies where we avoid talking about death, what comes after it, and how to manage grief. Bereavement is that terrible process that we all eventually face as we have to deal with the sudden and irrevocable loss of a loved one. Grief is not something that starts, gets better, and then we're over it. It is not linear. Instead, we may reach a point where we feel okay, only to have a sound, image, or thought rip our trembling legs out from under us, and we are right back at ground zero again. You are okay, and then you aren't.

Everyone's grief is unique, and no one can tell you to "get over it." There certainly isn't a time limit on grieving or on your bereavement. However, while it may feel like this has become your natural state of being, and that you will never again know life without grieving, you can reach a point where the grief is soothed so that it no longer dominates your life. It becomes a palatable, bittersweet sorrow that you need only acknowledge when necessary.

At this point, that may not seem like a blessing or even any comfort to you. Chances are that you just want life to return to normal, and if one more person tells you "I'm sorry" you feel like may actually explode! Well, this is normal too. This is the anger that comes after your initial loss. You see, grief has stages, and though this is little comfort to you right now, it will help you to not feel alone in your grief, and to know that at some point, your grief will subside.

Your process of trying to deal with grief has probably made you embark on a journey to find answers. The big question plaguing you is probably "Why?" Sadly, you may never find a satisfactory answer to this question; however, your searching has brought you here. This book can be your companion and guide on the journey to reach the other side of your grief.

This book will debunk some common myths about grieving that may be tripping you up and causing you more pain than you actually need to suffer. It will help you deal with feeling overwhelmed, and it will explain the stages of grief so that you can know what could come next on your journey, and how you can deal with each successive stage. As you progress on your journey through grief, you will also need to find ways to deal with all of the friends, family, and coworkers (those well-meaning people who want to check in on you), who ask questions, and who offer (often unhelpful) advice. This book will guide you through finding suitable responses to their questions, how to avoid questions, and how to deal with people who push in upon your personal relationship with your grief.

As life starts to return to "normal," you will also feel a desperate need for guidance on how to return to the normal things of life such as going back to work, dealing with family interactions, normal socializing, and the changes in your family and life structure. This book will also guide you on how to make decisions with clarity, explain what decisions to put on hold and why, as well as how to find a style of grieving that will work for you.

Finally, some of us are simply not able to move on alone, and this book will help you know when you should seek professional help, what to expect from that help, how to build a support network, and help you learn how to make decisions in life again now that that star that you revolved around has gone. Life keeps going, there is no end. There is only transition, and after traveling the journey of grief, you will be able to find happiness again. Though the star that you used to look at is no longer burning brightly, your own light still shines in the dark. Take my hand, and let's begin the journey through your grief.

Chapter 1:

In the Very Beginning–It's Normal

to Feel Numb

"In the garden of memory, in the palace of dreams...that is where you and I shall meet." Lewis Carroll, *Alice Through the Looking Glass*.

Losing someone is perhaps the single most traumatic experience that we all need to face in life. Someone we depended on, someone we loved, who we cared for, and turned to is suddenly gone. They continue living in our thoughts, dreams, and memories only. Being left behind means that you will need to find new ways to continue living, redefine your life, and decide on what happens to your relationship with the person you have lost.

When the pain is still so fresh, and you don't know how (never mind if) you will ever get through your grief, you may feel that you are destined to live in grief forever. You may even want to defend your right to do so. Loyalty may drive you to believe that you should grieve forever to honor the one you lost, and thanks to thousands of romantic poets, we tend to think it's romantic to "die of a broken heart." It isn't. And you still have the living to care for, be with, and account to. Your life is still there, and finding the inspiration and wisdom to live that life to the full despite the burden of sorrow that you bear is not always easy.

Grieving non-stop is not healthy, and you may end up doing as the poets wrote, and die of heart disease due to the physical toll of suffering from grief. Certainly, grief increases your chances of contracting a stress-sensitive disease such as heart failure, cancer, and diabetes. You may even be driven towards suicide by wanting to join the person that you have lost. Finding a reason to carry on despite and through your grief may be a real challenge to you. It is important at this point to tell you that you are not alone, and you are still loved and valued. There is a reason to rebuild your life and live on despite the sorrow that you are now struggling with.

On the journey through grief, you will also have to deal with many misconceptions regarding bereavement. For starters, it does not have a time limit, and you can't set a countdown clock for when your grief will end. Over time, you may end up feeling like your coping mechanisms are broken if you expect your grief to end within a certain amount of time. But all this comes later, for right now, as your grief starts, you may end up feeling only one thing: numb.

All I Felt Was Numb

My father died. Suddenly the pillar of my life was no longer there, but instead of screaming and crying like a baby, I felt nothing. There was only a huge numbness that covered my heart and mind. While everyone around me was falling apart, I seemed to be stuck in limbo, functioning like a machine. Soon I felt intense guilt. Did I not love my dad? Was I an unfilial child because I was unable to express my grief? What was wrong with me? It was only later that I discovered that being numb was a normal initial response to death and the start of grief. I did not have to feel guilty about being numb; it was normal. My refusal to start grieving or to even acknowledge that I had lost someone I held so dear were quite normal responses. I was only at the start of my grief journey.

In technical terms, this feeling of numbness is called anhedonia, and it refers to when you feel an absence of emotions despite the normal and even extreme triggers that should elicit an emotional response. This numbness is not taking the easy way out or avoiding the reality of grief as some people might say. Instead it feels awful. However, this is only the start of your journey.

It is also incredibly difficult to share how that numbness feels to people around you. They might say things like, "It's okay, you should let out your emotions" or "You'll feel better when you cry." And these comments are highly unhelpful. Those who stand outside of your grief have no concept of how painful feeling numb really is, or how little control you have over it. While grief is a universal experience, grieving reactions are not. While someone else may have been able to immediately begin crying and using their coping skills after they lost someone, they are not you. They will not have grieved the same way as you.

The numbness you may experience feels terrible. You feel as if you are the one who should die, and you feel like you are floating through the events of your life, completely divorced from all control and interest. With numbness, you feel like you are isolated from the people who care about you, and their attempts to help you can prove annoying or even barely register on you. Nothing makes sense, and the only sense of emotion that you may feel is guilt.

You not only feel guilty, but you also doubt your own feelings, or lack of them. Surely you should be able to cry when someone you love has died? Are you some kind of emotionless freak? A sociopath? You doubt all that you believed about yourself, and now you have to deal with self-deconstruction on top of your grief.

Despite people trying to help you, you simply can't "let it all out" or "grieve for the one you lost." How do you start when you are stuck in neutral? Pills don't help, and even therapy may be useless at this point. Strangely, the old adage of "time is a great healer" is quite true since your mind is struggling to start turning over the event that has so shocked and incapacitated you. Over time, you will begin to feel again, and you will move forward (even if you don't really move on, for the time being). However, be warned, the return of your emotions may be a tidal wave that may feel like it's going to drown you. Just hold on!

Why Bereavement Is Numbing

Even if you know that someone will die (as in a terminally ill person), you may still struggle to face up to the absence of that person from your life. The worst part is that death is something that you can't really see or fight against. You are left powerless.

The sudden and massive influx of feelings and fears that comes with the person's departure from your world can be hugely overwhelming. You doubt and feel like you are stuck in a dream, and wonder if it even happened. In some instances, you may even expect your loved one to show up again. This may be why the practice of viewing the body before the funeral has been a long-established custom in many cultures. For some, seeing the body is a type of closure to begin understanding their loss and their grief. Others may find that they fear looking at their loved one, and this may be a protective mechanism to try and avoid the trauma of their grief. This certainly ties in with the Kubler-Ross model of stages of grief. The first stage is denial, and numbness is the initial condition of grieving.

You may understand the theory behind grief on a mental level, but emotionally, you are unable to process the concept. No one can know what they will respond like in your situation, according to Royden (2019). Therefore, they can't speak for how you should react either, and they don't have the right to make comments on how you should react. Chances are good that you are feeling numb for a good reason: you are likely under so much pressure that if you were to begin your grieving process, you would have an emotional melt-down or blow your mind completely. Being numb may be your way of waiting until some of the pressure and negative energies have subsided so that you can then safely begin your grieving process.

To try and get through the bereavement process and to break down the feeling of numbness, some people try to elicit an emotional response by turning to activities that make them feel "alive" again such as extreme sports, excessive drinking and then picking fights, risky behavior, and even self-harming actions like self-mutilation, starving themselves, or over-eating. You might be tempted to try anything just to feel something, anything again.

This is the moment when you need to be kind to yourself. You're processing grief in your own time and way. No two people grieve in the same way or within the same amount of time. This is also not something that anyone can help you with initially. You simply need to wait for your mind to process everything and let it find ways to store and interpret what has happened. The sense of numbness is your mind's way of protecting you from feelings that you may not be ready to deal with yet. You may then find that you experience what is known as delayed grief much later, or a sudden and unexpected influx of emotions and memories about the person who you have lost. This may happen in stages, like a bubble that rises to the surface as you release the pressurized container of your own emotions.

These abrupt eruptions of emotions that come after the numbness may make you wish that you could have stayed numb forever; however, loss, anger, frustration, and confusion are merely the next progressions of the grief journey. Think of them as stops along the road to healing and adjusting.

Chapter 2:

You're Not Crazy: Loss, Anger, and Confusion As A Permanent State of Being

After those initial days, weeks, or even a month or two of feeling numb, hurting and not being able to express it, you may begin to think you have gone crazy as loss, anger, and confusion strike. Suddenly, and for no reason, you are angry at everyone, and you are confused by everything. Worse still, you seem to be angry and confused the whole time and about everything in your life. Guilt still creeps in, like almond essence taking over confectionary, flavoring your life with regret.

Helpful strangers offer advice, usually without even asking if you want any. On a daily basis, you may be offered these hugely unhelpful suggestions and beliefs about life, death, the after-life, and how to *deal* with it. If only those well-meaning people would realize that it's up to you to figure out. Which brings us to grieving myth, that long list of thoughts, quotes, and religious-minded "treasures" that people pass along to those who are new to the grief process.

Grieving Myths

These myths may make you feel worse and not better. They impose a timetable and structure for your grief upon you, and when you can't or won't meet it, you feel even worse and more guilty. Don't. Grief is *your* process, and no one has the right to tell you how, where, when, or if you should grieve. The sad reality is that we are not schooled about how to deal with death. It isn't a course we take at school, and we are woefully ill-equipped to deal with this part of life. And make no mistake, we all deal with death eventually.

The following myths about bereavement are completely false and unhelpful, so watch out for them:

- **Just Ignore Your Grief, It Will Go Away**

How sad, but people actually believe this. They mistakenly think that they should get back to the business of living, and their grief will magically disappear. Suppressing your pain will only worsen it. The pain from grief is like an abscess that needs to be opened and drained for healing to occur. Only once you have removed the thorn that is festering in you, can you begin to heal and then move on. As with wounds, sometimes you will have to reopen a wound to heal completely. Healing demands that you invest time and care into the grieving process. Ignoring it will only cause delayed grief and make your pain fester in you. Grief will not heal without leaving a scar though, but that is okay. Scars are signs that you are living and that you are continuing to live despite the pains that you have suffered.

- **Adults Don't Cry**

Why is it that once you are all grown up, you suddenly lose the right to cry? Everyone has the right to cry, and in some cases, it may even help those around you to release their sorrow when they see you cry. Medically speaking, crying releases hormones that detoxify the body, and it increases the production of serotonin, a neurotransmitter that helps you to feel better. This is why after having a good cry, you may actually feel better than you did before. Even though you may not be able to cry during the numb phase, you might feel yourself drawn to tears later during the grieving process. Believing that you are an adult and you shouldn't cry because it may upset your family is not going to help you manage your grief. Instead, you should be able to cry. Expressing yourself physically with tears is healthy for you and may help your family.

- **When You Don't Cry, You Aren't Grieving**

Tears are not the only ways to deal with grief. Some people choose to turn their energies to remembering the person they lost, moving on by reflecting and cherishing their memories. Judging someone for not crying is extremely arrogant, and it's hugely unhelpful.

- **Feeling Numb Isn't Normal**

It is quite normal and more common than you think for people to feel numb at the beginning of grief. Not everyone launches into the grieving process immediately. Sometimes it is normal for the feeling of numbness to be there to ease you into grieving and dealing with bereavement. Believing that being numb is abnormal is not only harmful but can cause complications when dealing with your grief as it adds to your guilt load.

- **Grieving Takes Four Years**

There are many myths about how long it takes to recover or fully grieve for the loss of a loved one. Some psychologists believe this process to be finalized after four years; however, this is another fallacious belief. No one can set a time limit to your grief. Anyone who tries is being insensitive; they don't walk in your shoes, and they don't lead your life. How dare they tell you that it's long enough now.

- **You Must be Going Crazy**

When you have lost someone, the grieving process may be so overwhelming that you become forgetful, emotionally unstable, and short on concentration. You may lose sleep, stop functioning and reasoning rationally, and people may begin to think that you must be going crazy. You aren't. Your brain is merely processing everything that has happened. Losing someone often happens without any warning, and this tumultuous feeling is normal when grieving. This feeling of being crazy will pass, you have not lost your marbles.

- **Work Through the Stages of Grief From A to B, and You Will Be Fine**

We tend to think about life as being linear. We are born, we live, and then we die. However, grief is not a linear process. It loops backwards and for every step you take towards closure, you may slide back two. Grief is more of an organic circular process where you work through the stages of grief, but you may find yourself returning to address issues later on that you had maybe brushed over. You can't see the different stages as milestones that you pass and leave in the rearview mirror.

- **Men Don't Grieve as Much**

There is a misconception that people still cling to that men grieve less than women. Perhaps this is because women are more inclined to publicly express their grief by crying, while men tend to grieve on the inside and in private. However, there is no measure of grief, and it is ridiculous to presume that men grieve less than women. This fallacious belief may cause conflict between people where they may mistakenly think that their partner is not grieving the loss as much as they do. We especially see this when a couple has lost a child. Just because the man does not cry and openly express how they feel does not mean that they grieve the loss of their child any less than their female partner does.

- **Grief Shouldn't Affect Your Relationships**

Often people believe that grief should unite them with their partners or family members. However, the reality is a far cry from this. Often grief is a destructive force in relationships, and the guilt that the partners in the relationship feel may become projected onto the other party, resulting in the violent end of the relationship. Families also break apart when they are not able to respect each other's grieving process. Holding onto mistaken beliefs about grief and bereavement may also contribute to the conflict that actual loss causes in a relationship.

- **When You Grieve, You Don't Smile**

Grief is not a jug that pours and pours until it is empty. It's rather like a leaky boat that seem to be sinking for a moment then floats again, and in between there are moments when you are not grieving. In those moments, you are who you have always been. If you smile, laugh, and joke, you are still someone who is grieving. You are just not grieving in that moment. Biologically, our bodies often respond after crying with a smile or a laugh. Remember that our bodies are wired to recover equilibrium. It will balance intense sorrow with moments of levity. There is nothing wrong with having those gaps when you can breathe and be human. Yet, people often judge and believe that you should take grieving seriously. You may even judge yourself and feel guilty when you feel a moment of happiness during your grief. Smiling doesn't mean that you aren't doing just that. After all, grieving is about adjusting, remembering, and living on. Sorrow comes in waves, and in between, you can swim instead of sinking.

- **You Can't Grieve the Loss of an Animal**

"Are you crazy? It's just a dog." We have all had someone say something like this when we are grieving the loss of a beloved pet. Yet society still does not fully understand or support the grieving that follows the death of a pet or other loved animal. Often the loss of a beloved animal can even lead to depression when people are unable to successfully mourn their loss. Any living being that you have developed strong feelings over has made an impact on your life and your mind. Losing an animal is just as painful and in need of grieving as losing a family member.

Often our misconceptions of grief and our implied judgments can cause greater harm to people dealing with grief than their pain can. If you want to help someone who is grieving, you should respect their grief process which will probably be very different from your own. Different cultures also grieve in different ways. In a culturally diverse world, we should take cognizance of this. The Irish have wakes that resemble a party, while the Japanese view death as an honor and something to celebrate. In Hindu cultures, it is quite normal to include the deceased in their continuing family rituals, and modern-day Hindus may even have a deceased family member digitally added to their new family photos.

Being Overcome

Losing someone is a traumatic experience, regardless of which culture you come from. And though people have different notions about how to honor the dead and how to lay them to rest, the final grieving is a personal process. Certainly, you can expect to feel overcome with emotions like shock, despair, anger, fear, and guilt.

Being overcome is natural. Anyone who tells you differently is not being realistic. Your world has stopped, and it now spins off the cantle as someone who had occupied a space in your life is no longer there. You need to rediscover how to move forward even if you can't move on yet.

What is interesting is that the concept of overcome has two opposing meanings. Firstly, it means to be overwhelmed and to lose all emotional control; secondly, it means to win through something, to move past something. So while you may feel overcome in the sense of being unable to take even a single step forward, you can also overcome and simply try to raise your emotional foot, even if you can't step.

Being emotionally overcome can be truly damaging to your own life. This often happens when we are so intertwined in the life of the person we have lost that we no longer know how to lead a life of our own. A brilliant example of this is the 1996 movie *To Gillian on Her 37th Birthday*. In this touching film, the main character is trying to deal with being completely overcome by his wife's tragic death. His struggle to come to terms with grieving her loss has resulted in him having hallucinations where he sees his dead wife. Being overcome to the point of having a physiological reaction is not healthy, and it may lead to real-life dangers and a complete mental breakdown.

This movie also shows a typical example of well-meaning relatives who try to prescribe how to grieve to the widowed father. When you are overcome emotionally, it is up to you to figure out how to overcome your grief.

The Difference Between Grief and Mourning

You may now begin to understand that you are entering a pathway that lets you travel with your loss in a process of grieving. This is a necessary part of the journey, and it allows you to begin to process your feelings, start to experience life without the person you have lost, and acknowledge the range of feelings and memories that you have about that person. The grief at the loss of someone special may never go away.

Once you start to carry on with your normal life, you may begin to find a new way to maintain the presence of that person in your life, either as a memory or as someone who you honor for having been a part of your life. Just because they have died does not mean that you must now cut them out of your life indefinitely. Perhaps this is why grief is not meant to simply disappear. This process of reintegration of your life with your grief is what we call mourning. It is when you are ready to speak about your loss from within your new life.

Grief mostly happens on the inside, and it is incredibly hard to express at times. Mourning is what happens on the outside, what you choose to show to the other people in our life about how you are processing life beyond a loved one's death. When you are ready to carry a beloved person's death as part of your life, not as a moment when your life (or theirs) stopped, but as a genuine part of your life, you have moved into mourning. Contrary to popular belief, mourning is not some milestone that you accomplish, and then magically you are over grieving.

The concept of mourning is often seen as a (limited) tragic and negative time for you and your family. That could not be further from the truth. Mourning is supposed to be a time when you grow beyond and *with* your pain. It is when you acknowledge the full scope of your grief and let yourself naturally move through it (as many times as is necessary). Mourning is about feeling sorrow for the loss that you have experienced, and it may trigger feelings of guilt. You are living, and they are not. Focusing your grief on feeling sorrow and pain is a process that may disempower you since it has little forward momentum. You simply feel the sorrow. Mourning means that you take action, you integrate the grief and the sorrow, and you build forward momentum.

When Sorrow Carries Guilt

When you have lost someone who mattered to you, grieving is a natural symptom. Your grief will inevitably lead to sorrow, and that sorrow carries a measure of guilt. It's like you blame yourself for being sad, for not bouncing back, or carrying on like everyone else seems to be doing. You perceive yourself as being weak or being emotionally shut off when you struggle to release the emotions that you may be busy repressing.

The range of myths that we discussed earlier may only contribute to your sense of shame and guilt, worsening your sorrow and ultimately halting the healing (or dealing) process. It also does not help when you attend therapy only to be told that you are not working through your feelings when really, you are trying.

Sorrow and the grief that you are experiencing is a fluid process, and while you may be fine one minute, you might not be okay the next. These moments of being okay and then suddenly not being able to cope can create feelings of remorse. You may feel like you had not brought your share to the relationship with the person you lost. Regret leads to a constant replay of what happened and then not being able to make peace with the past.

You may desire closure since this would seem to be the end of your conflict and remorse replays. While you desire for the grief to end, you may be clinging to it since it is the only substitute that you now have in lieu of the person you lost. You could be overcome by the feeling that you did not spend enough time with your loved one. As a result, you could end up punishing yourself for not being there for the one who passed.

This is, however, a view in the rearview mirror, and you did the best you could with what was available to you. Once you begin to understand that closure is not about letting yourself "off the hook" but rather about finding a way to cope, you will be able to initiate the grieving process and eventually integrate your grief with your life through a process of mourning.

The Weight of Sorrow

Now that you know of the complexity of the burden that comes with sorrow and grieving, you may begin to understand why sorrow can make you feel at times as if you can't breathe. It is like carrying a weight on your heart that seems to squeeze the life right out of you: suddenly the world seems grey, and you lack the strength to even smile.

This is the weight of sorrow, and for many, it can be so overwhelming that they struggle to put one foot in front of the other or get out of bed in the morning. Some who are busy grieving struggle to be around those they love, and they don't want to or can't continue with a normal life. Everything they do and everywhere they go remind them of who they lost.

So how do you carry the weight of your sorrow?

- **Accept It**

When you are sad, you may want to not be so. You may wish that all of that pain and sorrow could just disappear; it won't. As soon as you accept that you may be sad on and off for the rest of your life, you can start to move through that pain. You can then start to acknowledge that sorrow is only one aspect of your life: it need not be the whole of your life.

- **Give Yourself Time**

You need to show yourself the same amount of patience and respect that you would give another person who is grieving. You wouldn't tell someone else to hurry up and get over it, so don't tell yourself to. Take as much time as you need to grieve. Spread it out, there is no rush, and you don't have to consume and digest all of your grief on a weekend so that you can be bright and shiny at work on Monday. Know that you don't have to bounce back, and you can take as much time and guidance as you need or want.

- **Find Your Trigger**

Most of us will have a trigger that seems to be hard-wired into our emotions. You have something that sets you off, causing a massive emotional eruption that makes it seem as if the person you loved died all over again. If you can identify the triggers that cause you to travel back into your memories, where you struggle to remember without suffering, then you can avoid that which causes you pain now.

You may have to avoid certain places and events that are still too painful for you to cope with. And that's okay. Over time, you will be able to prepare for a known trigger, and it won't affect you too harshly.

- **Look for the Bright Spark**

Regardless of how dark and miserable days following the death of your loved one are, you can still look up. Not everyone likes to think of this as some religious experience, but instead, it is about finding the joy in life. Yes, joy still remains, even though you have been blindfolded by grief. With some time and by focusing on each moment on its own, you can also find the bright spark that shows you how life still carries on. You are still a part of it, and you can shine and enjoy the bright beauty of your friends and family who are there to walk the road with you. You are not alone.

- **Talk About It**

This is a hard one for many people. How do you talk about it when you don't know what to say? Who should you talk to? Professionals are a great help here, but even a complete stranger can do (even though it may be a little awkward). It doesn't need to be a flood of words, even letting out a few words about your loss and how you are grieving is a great help. And if there is no one who you can turn to, you can talk to a tree, or even hug an animal. This is about hearing your own voice saying the things that you are feeling. It is not about the other person offering your advice.

By saying your feelings aloud, you acknowledge them, and this is important. You might even consider talking to the memory of the person who has died. In a way, this might be therapeutic as they knew you so well, making long explanations unnecessary. A great example of this technique in practice is shown in the 2005 movie *Elizabethtown*, where a son has to deal with his father's passing. In this instance, the son takes a road trip with his dad's ashes, scattering it at all the places they would have seen together. After sharing his feelings with a complete stranger who he meets, the son also engages in discussions with his dad's memory. Healing takes whichever form is most relevant to you.

- **Accept Care, Not Help**

You need support. Although the process of mourning is your own, you do not need to go through it alone. There are people in your life who care about you, whether friends or family or complete strangers who you interact with occasionally–you do not exist alone. People care about you. Accept their care, even if you don't want their help.

You may feel really lost at this stage of the grieving process, and you may even long for someone to tell you what to do or where to go. Give yourself time. Accept that this is about feeling, not about doing. You don't have to be better or magically get over anything. Life as you know it has changed, and you need to find a way to cope, to be you, and to be okay (most of the time). You do not need to accept what others believe about grief; instead, find what works for you. Don't be afraid to ask for help when you can't move forward anymore, but also accept that it is okay to just idle here in this moment for a while. Grief is a process, a marathon, not a sprint.

Chapter 3:

The Stages of Grief Theory

We have an insatiable need to understand things that affect us on a grand and life-changing scale, and for this reason, there have been many theories that have attempted to explain the different stages that grief can be divided into. Some of these theories have up to seven stages an individual needs to go through to reach the point of closure. Perhaps the most iconic is the Kubler-Ross model of grief.

The Kubler-Ross Model of Grief

Originally created by psychiatrist Elizabeth Kübler-Ross in her book, *On Death and Dying*, following her work with terminally ill patients, this model mapped the most common stages that people move through after the loss of a loved one. One drawback of this theory is that people mistakenly believe that you simply tick off each stage and then reach the goal of closure at the end in a predefined time period. Nothing could be further from the truth though.

In the application of this theory, it becomes clear that not everyone will experience their grief in the same order of stages, nor may everyone even experience all the different stages. Those suffering through the grief process may also circle back from one stage to a previously experienced stage, depending on their own emotional state and the way in which their grief reacts to their attempts to mourn and cope.

It is useful to know the theory of the stages of grief, not because it predetermines how you will feel next, but to help you identify how you might be feeling now, and prepare you for what may come next. The five stages model is useful as a guide to help you not feel as isolated or alone in your grief, though you may experience each stage of grief in your own unique way.

Denial

Perhaps one of the most universal of all emotions is to feel denial when we are informed of the tragic loss of someone we love. It is an emotion that is designed to protect you, and in denying that it happened, you hope to spare yourself the pain that you subconsciously know is coming. Numbness is often a close runner-up to denial, and you may feel this as your emotions become strained, and you feel overwhelmed. Feeling numb is also your mind's way to create time and space to better process or cope with everything that has happened.

In this stage of the grief process, you may say something like, "No, it didn't happen. She/he isn't gone. It isn't happening." You will be trying to protect yourself, defend against the feeling of loss, and you may even deny that it is affecting you at all, leading to isolation. The resulting numbness that you may then feel, rises like a buffer that isolates you from the world and the pain that you are not ready to acknowledge.

However, when you are ready to start acknowledging how you feel and the traumatic truth that happened, you could begin to experience emotions such as anger and rage, and fatalistic life views. This may signal the shift to another stage of grief namely, anger.

What To Do During the Denial Stage:
- **Give Yourself Time**

When the loss has occurred, you need to give yourself time. There is no clock that times what is the appropriate length of time to feel numb or to be in denial. Take as much time as is necessary for you to feel ready to move on.

- **Think About Them and Talk About Them**

While your mind is processing what happened, you should try to naturally think about the person you have lost. Don't dwell on the loss, instead, think about the good times together and what they meant to you. This will create warmth and positive energy to carry you forward. Though you may have lost someone special, you have not lost your time with them.

- **Ask Questions When You Feel Ready**

When you are ready, ask questions about what happened. Don't let yourself get buried under what if's. Instead try to remain focused on what happened in reality and what you can do now. This can be difficult, especially when the person died in a traumatic way. Try to direct your questions in a positive way, and accept the answers you receive (at least at first). It serves no purpose to know whether someone suffered in a car accident before dying, so try not to dwell on those questions now.

Anger

For some people, the initial denial is followed by a stage of anger. Whether directed at others or themselves, anger is often the way in which people who grieve mask the depth of their own very painful emotions. It is another protection mechanism from the human mind, and it is a way to play for time to let the full message of grieving and loss sink into your mind.

You may feel angry at external forces, such as your god for taking someone from you; you may even be angry at the person who died for not taking better care of themselves. This anger may be expressed verbally or through actions, and it can be incredibly upsetting to your family to see. For this reason, many people who grieve turn their anger inwards, avoiding expressing it, and they walk around with incredibly negative energy in them that others can sense, and that makes the person grieving suffer alone.

If you are in this stage of grieving, you may even wonder what earthly purpose anger could serve, and the answer may be simpler than you think. Anger means that you can remain defensive and not have to reveal your vulnerable side to the world (or to yourself). You can rather convince yourself that the person who died, their doctor, or the world is to blame, not you.

This anger may manifest as resentment or even self-blame. You wonder what you could have done to save them, and thoughts about this may end up torturing you: "If only I had been driving" or "I should have insisted that Dad quit smoking years ago" or "I should never have hired a sitter or gone on that date."

Many people may never experience this stage acutely, and it may blend in with the stage of denial, where they will alternate between feeling numb and being angry. The results will be the same though, a mental avoidance of your real feelings or delay until you are ready to fully acknowledge how you are feeling.

While anger is easier to express than sorrow or pain, it does keep other people at a distance, and it can be damaging to your health in the long run. Anger does have strong medical ties to heart attacks and strokes. Though anger may seem easier to feel than other emotions, it is not productive, and if it continues for more than a few days or weeks, you may need to seek help from either a friend or a mental health professional who you feel comfortable talking to. You should not deny your anger, and you have every right to feel angry, however, you should not let it hold you back from your grief for so long that anger becomes your habit.

What To Do During the Anger Stage:

- **Give Yourself Permission to be Angry**

When you feel angry, it is okay. Say that to yourself over and over. We are conditioned by society to believe that anger is not acceptable. But your anger over the death of someone you loved is not about being acceptable; it is about you, and how you are feeling at each moment. You are starting to feel, and while you may be angry right now, you may finally begin to feel sorrow and grieve in the next moment. Accept that you can only get there by allowing your anger to run its course.

- **Voice How Angry You Are**

It is important to find your voice during this stage. People will be offering condolences and advice that may be helpful or not, but you need to be able to respond to these when you feel the anger build. Don't wait until you can't bear it anymore and then explode at the person. Once your anger passes, you will still want to be friends with those people, and you will need a support network going forward. Feel your anger and speak it out as calmly as you can. Telling someone that you value their advice, but that you are not feeling the same way as they did is acceptable. Screaming at someone to go to hell when they've only told you how sorry they are, is not acceptable. Speaking as you feel will lessen the emotional pressure of your anger. Share your feelings where possible.

- **Find Forgiveness**

This is an incredibly difficult feeling or state to accomplish. However, it is really important and ongoing. During this stage of anger, try to find some sense of forgiveness for yourself, for the deceased, for those who are trying to support you and end up saying the wrong thing, and for the situation that claimed your loved one's life. This ongoing process of forgiveness is central to the grief stages and integrating yourself into mourning. It is about giving yourself and others a small measure of grace from one moment to the next, even if it's only a thimble-full at a time.

Bargaining

Once the anger begins to fade or the numbness of denial thaws somewhat, you may enter another stage – bargaining. During this stage, you may try to reclaim some feeling of being in control by engaging in bargaining thoughts. This is also a way to deny what has happened and to avoid dealing with or facing the full emotional flood of your feelings. You try to rationalize what has happened, and by bargaining, you try to avoid the inevitable sense of loss that you feel during grief.

During the mourning process, you may try to bargain so that you can avoid your sorrow, and to try and regain a sense of control over a situation that you have absolutely no control over. In the end, we do not control death. We can only control how we respond to it once we have allowed ourselves to embrace the grieving process and integrate this with our lives in mourning.

You may find yourself thinking or saying things like "I promise to stop smoking if you let him live," (if your loved one is dying) or "If I had paid more attention, I would have seen the signs." With these questions, you direct the blame inward, believing that you could somehow have prevented the death and loss of your loved one. You may feel like you should be punished for not being able to save the person who died, and you could end up punishing yourself. This kind of helpless reasoning leads to more guilt, and the process of grieving may circle back on itself, running through numbness and anger again.

What To Do During the Bargaining Stage:

- **Let Go of False Hope**

During this stage of the grieving process, you may cling to false hope. This is especially true when the person you are grieving for is terminally ill, in a coma, or has just died. It is important not to create false hope in yourself during this stage, as this will only delay the inevitable acceptance that life ends. Death comes when we least expect it, and there is nothing that you can do to change that.

- **Talk to Others**

When you are bargaining in your mind, you may not realize just how unrealistic your thoughts are. However, if you can speak about them to someone else, or even just say these thoughts out loud, you may find yourself naturally letting go of unrealistic hopes.

- **Ride the Rollercoaster**

Prepare yourself for a rollercoaster ride of emotions as you may be circling between bargaining and getting angry when you realize that you can't bargain, to then feeling numb and shut-down before you try to bargain again. This is normal. Your brain is processing. You might try an affirmation at this point, or create a personal motto to help you release the illusion of control during a bargaining phase. By saying something like "Just let go" you might be able to show yourself some kindness and weather the storm better.

Depression

When you have begun to let go of bargaining, and your anger begins to fade, you will find yourself fully present in the now. With this presence, you may find that this now (without the person you have lost) is lonely and empty. Naturally, you may find yourself sinking into a feeling of depression. The reality without the person you lost stinks. That's right, it stinks. Very few of us will approach the loss of someone with cheering, so it's normal for you to not like what you see in life without the person who made your world spin. After all, this emptiness is what depression is all about, isn't it?

Introspection is quite normal now as you try to figure out if life can or should work without the person you lost. You may isolate yourself while you try to process and redefine who you are without that presence in your life. Sadness may develop to even larger proportions and crying is something that may happen often. This is a biological response of your body to try and soothe you; don't be ashamed of it or try to avoid it. Crying is an expression of your sorrow.

You have finally stopped dodging your emotions through denial, anger, and bargaining. In this stage, you have begun to really feel and process the loss you have suffered, and you may truly be suffering through this stage. Prepare yourself for a messy and hectic experience. Depression is not a pretty place to be, but now that you have begun to truly grieve, it is a necessary place for you to emotionally and mentally be in.

What is important to note is that this depression is natural, and though it may seem like it will last forever, it is necessary for you to feel this way following the tragedy of loss. Not being depressed after having a loved one die would be inappropriate and deviant.

It is difficult to say how long one should take to feel this sense of depression, and it will differ from person to person; however, if your depression begins to consume your life and interferes with your ability to live, you should consider seeking professional help. It may be tempting to medicate with antidepressants to feel better, and many people who support the grieving process will oppose this idea, but we are both emotional and biological organisms. This means that for some of us, the chemical reactions of our grief may require outside interventions to prevent our depression from becoming a result of (or triggering) a chemical imbalance.

What To Do During the Depression Stage:

- **Know That It Will End**

Kübler-Ross wrote that it may help to see depression as a visitor who comes despite you not liking them (Love Lives On.com, n.d.)

- **Find Help**

Though you may be focusing on yourself during this stage, it need not be a lonely journey. You can find help in the form of friends, family, counselors, online platforms, and other professionals. Even though you may not feel like turning to people for help, you should find help when necessary. Don't try to tough it out as this will only make you suffer more.

- **Create Structure**

Now that you have suddenly lost that pivotal person to death, you may feel like you are confused and unsure about life moving forward or how to look backward. Creating structure by finding people to support you, and events or tasks that help you to feel like you have meaning. Schedule meetings with friends, even though you may be feeling sad. Attend events that you used to like, even though they may remind you of the one you lost. Counter that loss by remembering the better days instead of focusing on the pain of being alone now.

- **Explore New Roads**

By introducing new things to do or explore, you create a new life story without the person you have lost. It is not about denying the person who has died, but rather, it is about finding and building forward momentum. This is hugely beneficial since it helps you to realize that depression is not a permanent state. It will come and go, and in between, you will continue on.

Acceptance

It's all over...no, it isn't. It is a common misconception that reaching the acceptance stage means that you have put your grief way behind you and moved on. Nothing could be further from the truth. Acceptance is not the final stage of your grief. It is not the finish line. You may not even be feeling okay.

Acceptance is about living onwards instead of inwards or backward. You have found your feet in the mourning process, and you are able to continue living productively. Your thinking paradigm shifts and you begin to allow yourself to open to new possibilities and embrace change.

There may still be numerous sad days when you may even go through some of the earlier stages such as anger or moments of denial. The difference is that you have now learned to deal with these and can see them as transient moments. While much of your life has changed, you are able to function from one day to the next. You may not be able to plan your life for next year, but can any of us ever do that anyway? The important thing is that you know that you can be okay, even if you are not okay at this moment right now.

What To Do During the Acceptance Stage:

- **The New Norm**

The old you has changed during the stages of grief, and in this stage of acceptance, you need to find a new norm for yourself. Your concept of what is normal for you will have to be rearticulated by your mind during the acceptance process by redefining and accepting the new you, your new roles, and what you can allow and want to have in your life.

- **Show Patience**

You will be feeling quite uncertain about a lot of things, and your acceptance will be carrying you forward. Accept that in this stage you will be making mistakes, as you are re-learning and you are exploring. This takes patience, and you should show yourself and the people in your life a little kindness.

Limitations of the Stages of Grief Model

If you feel that the five stages of grief model may not be for you, chances are that you are right. So why include it in this book? It is a starting point to find a way to manage your grief, however, your personal approach to your own grief will require modification according to your unique needs.

There are limitations to the stages of grief model. Firstly, it is probably outdated. Nothing in life remains completely relevant for more than a few years. Even dictionaries get revised every couple of years. This particular theory on how to cope with grief is over half a century old at the time of this publication. Surely a lot has changed since it was first released. Yet, there are no revisions of the original model, no versions 2.0 to help the newer generations in applying this theory to help them deal with their grief.

In addition, the original objection to this theory has not changed. The five stages of grief model was designed in response and from information gathered in dealing with people who were terminally ill and are facing the grief of their own imminent death. Over the last 50 years, psychologists have done heaps more research in dealing with clients who are facing grief following the direct loss of a loved one. This has given rise to many other theories on how to approach and cope with grief.

Yet, the stages of grief model remains popular, being immortalized in many Hollywood movies that deal with death and dying. Even people who are not psychologists can probably recite the five stages from what they have seen reflected in pop culture. Oh, certainly, this model has its uses, but it is not the alpha and omega of grief theories.

It has limits to how effective it can be. For instance, it creates a false sense of certainty in a very uncertain time during grieving. It tricks people into believing it is a kind of checklist: "Check, I've done denial, been angry, tried to bargain, and felt depressed, and now I'll be okay, and I'll accept this death and move on." In reality, it isn't that simple. These stages are more like facets of a jewel, and only in certain instances will you see or experience a particular facet, or stage. Even after reaching a stage of acceptance, this acceptance may only be one part of your grief. In fact, you could experience anger and depression about someone's passing away again. This theory creates an unrealistic expectation of the grieving process when it is viewed as the rungs on a ladder.

Scientific studies have also questioned the notion of grief always having discernible stages according to Robert A. Neimeyer, an American psychologist and researcher (Shermer, 2008). It would be closer to the truth to see these five stages like soup ingredients that you stir in the pot of life, and every now and again, you ladle up a particularly flavored spoonful of something that you may be experiencing at that point in time.

So why do we persist in using and referring to this model and does it have any value today? We need to tell a story to make sense of our lives. This need to narrate our lives and find a meaningful conclusion is so strong that psychologists use it in therapy too. The five stages model is more like a set of landmarks or pivotal events that we can choose to see and include in our own story. They give a bit of structure to our experiences.

Unfortunately, when people experience grief and try to apply the five stages model theory exactly to their story, they may become disillusioned and feel they are grieving unsuccessfully when they miss one stage or don't feel any progress is made in their grief process. This can give rise to despair.

When you understand that the five stages model is more like five suggestions or pointers to keep an eye out for in your journey through (and with) grief, you can use it successfully as an aid to help you grieve and begin to mourn.

How to Use the Stages of Grief Model Successfully

Grieving is a personal journey. No two people do it the same. But a little direction can sometimes be helpful. This is where the five stages of grief model is valuable. If you understand that it is a guide, not a measure, you will benefit from it.

The key takeaways from the theory are that grief is temporary, but no one can tell you how long it could or should take. It is okay to feel numb when you experience grief. It is how your brain protects you from feelings that may be too overwhelming. And it is also okay to become angry. Grief is not fair. Death is not fair, but you will learn to cope with it. You will also learn that you have no power or control over grief (or death) and bargaining is nothing more than a delaying tactic of your brain. Following this model, you will realize that it is okay to feel depressed and sad over the loss you have suffered. After all, we all know that we *suffer* loss, we don't enjoy it. Lastly, you will learn that acceptance of your grief doesn't mean that it's okay now. It will probably never be *okay*; instead, you will begin to move forward, making that sorrow a part of your life in the mourning process.

There may be a whole range of other emotions that you will feel, including guilt, regret, resentment, remorse, and even relief (if you had to say goodbye to someone who was suffering). The five stages model helps and is useful in guiding you through a grieving process that may take many different forms. At least when you start to understand that grief isn't just experienced and then thrown away: it is a journey that involves many people including you (the person grieving), the deceased, and those who are trying to help and support you (your friends, family, and community members).

Chapter 4:

Alternative Theories of Grief

There are a great many different approaches and theories to grief throughout the world's psychology circles, not to mention the religious views that abound and have diverse uptakes on death and dealing with it. These theories should be considered as differing views on death, dying, and the grieving process. Though you might not find any of these to answer your questions in their entirety, you can certainly benefit from the diverse views, making up an approach to bereavement that helps you to cope and form the skills you need to get through each day, whether it is a good day or a bad day.

Beyond The Kubler-Ross Stages

The criticisms of the Kubler-Ross stages theory have pointed out that grief is never as neat as a linear movement through five stages. Certainly, there are other theories that have as many as seven stages or as few as two stages, however, people grieve in an organic and uniquely shaped way that is determined by their background, support systems, previous experience with grief, and their own strength of character.

Everyone will find a way to grieve that works for them. Indeed, you may experience all of the Kubler-Ross stages jumbled together in a messy mix while you find your feet through your grieving process. In the end, the focus is on being able to cope with your grief, remain functional in your daily life, and eventually be able to lead a fulfilling life again.

What the Kubler-Ross and many other theories on grief do not adequately address is that the first year of grief is often a time of not only adjusting to life without the person you lost, but also a time of simply learning to survive without their financial and other means of support. If the person you lose suffered a prolonged illness, you may spend much time after their death simply trying to manage their medical expenses and dealing with a complicated estate. It is quite conceivable that after the initial numbness of losing someone, you may scurry around trying to deal with the practical aspects of living without that person for as much as a year. The second year of bereavement may result in an emotional rollercoaster as you suddenly begin to process emotions that you had previously pushed onto the backburner. Certainly, grief may not be something that can or should end. Instead, you may find that it is an evolutionary process that takes and then gives back to you in unexpected ways.

Grief Trajectory

As previously mentioned, grief is not a linear process. It is more of a circular process where you may be okay today and get all messed up when you run across a memory tomorrow that brings your grief forward again. Grief seems to have a trajectory that moves from focusing on how you are feeling to what you are doing to cope.

This means that you move from dealing with a range of emotions such as anger, sorrow, regret, blame, guilt, and fear to dealing with activities and tasks that require solutions such as funeral arrangements, working, living alone, and reallocating roles within the family.

Generally, men tend to focus on tasks as a means for coping, while women are more given to their emotional sensation of grief. Neither of these is more important than the other. You should learn to cope with emotions as well as learning to deal with the activities of living. The two aspects are intertwined. In understanding how this may affect different people within the grief circle, you will be able to support and help each other.

A couple that loses a child may have different reactions to grief and trying to cope. The husband may want to go out and do something to deal with their loss, while the wife may want to sit quietly, turning to introspection as she tries to make sense of how she feels. Conflict can arise if they don't each value the other's grieving process. Yet, their individual grieving can help each other. The wife could share her journaling to help her husband express what emotions he is struggling to deal with, and he may help her take actions to release her emotions.

The trajectory of your grief may not run in a continuous line either. While you may have an initial emotional reaction to the loss, you may be fine for several weeks, months, and even years, only to have something trigger emotions that you had been completely unaware of. This happens more often than not. Random events may trigger grief that may be as intense as if the person you are mourning had died anew.

Losing a child may resurface as intense sorrow during your friend's baby shower years later. What we are starting to realize is that grief does not go away. It may fade and become more bearable, but it always remains in your memories along with the person you are grieving for.

We tend to run from grief since it is such a painful emotion. You can't run from something that you carry with you though. The only way to conquer grief is to move through it, make peace with it, and reach an understanding of what grief tells you about life. Acceptance of your own experience with grief is not only soothing but also enriching. You will learn more about yourself and about those around you from grief and how you handle it than you will in an entire lifetime of *Pleasantville* happiness.

In our modern culture, where the focus is on doing and having, we want to have closure, to draw a line that neatly ends the experience of grief. This may be why we think that grief is something to get over. It isn't. Fortunately, there is a new mode of thinking about grief that is becoming popular where the experience of loss may be a result of death, but it doesn't mean the end of a relationship with the person who has died. This need not necessarily refer to a religious view of thinking of your loved one on the *other side*. Instead, it refers to acknowledging that the memories, feelings, experiences, and impact of that person does not end with their life. They live in your memories. That relationship can possibly continue beyond the grave. The extent of the relationship with a deceased person is entirely up to you, and you can work on that relationship still, even past death.

Psychologist J. W. Worden supports this view and believes that grief is work (Carney, 2020). It is a series of tasks that you can put effort into to reach the natural flow of your own grief process.

- **Accept the Reality of Loss**

In Worden's first stage, you accept that someone has died. This is when you admit to yourself that the person you have lost is truly gone. Viewing the body, dealing with the funeral, and selecting a tombstone are all pieces of the first task. The emotions of denial and anger are part of this task, and you aim to acknowledge them as being normal feelings to have when someone passes away. However, it is important to acknowledge that the person is truly no longer living. There is no negotiation and denial should be settled into acceptance of a new reality that forms after losing someone.

- **Grief and Pain**

In Worden's second stage, you focus on the pain and sorrow that comes with grief. The focus is on feeling all the emotions that you may feel following the acceptance of death. Pain, sorrow, anger, bitterness, and guilt can make up this stage. Activities such as journaling and group therapy sessions are ideal here to help express feelings. It is not about getting over how you are feeling. Instead, you should let yourself feel every emotion to the full. This is surprisingly hard work as our instinct is to protect ourselves from pain, thus we tend to deny our emotions.

- **Adjust to the New World**

Once you have expressed and experienced most of your emotions, you may begin to enter the third stage in the bereavement process: forming and accepting a world where the person who died is no longer there. This stage can often be filled with practical considerations such as work, changes in financial status, moving home, allocating new responsibilities within the family, and creating new habits and rituals.

Apart from coping at this stage of your mourning, you also realize the full scope of your loss as you discover all the little ways in which the person who died was a part of your life. It is important to understand this as you will begin to redefine who you are now.

- **Forming a New Relationship With the Deceased**

Worden's stages are unique in that they culminate in not only finding a way to move forward but also in forming a new relationship with the person who died. This acknowledges that the deceased do not leave our lives with their passing. We carry memories of them with us through the rest of our lives. It is up to us to redefine our relationship with those memories of the dead. This will impact our experience with grief. Much of our sorrow comes not from having lost someone but from not acknowledging them as being a part of our lives in the first place.

Establishing habits to remember them by is not only about honoring their memory but also about giving ourselves permission to be sad. Going to visit their graves is not about only respecting their memory but also about grieving. It is a way to process grief and acknowledge the impact of the relationship with our memories of the person we have lost.

If you tend to get angry when someone tells you to get *over* your loss or to seek *closure*, then this view might sit better with your own grief process. It acknowledges that love transcends all boundaries, even death. Just because someone has died does not mean that they are gone. Grief is not something that ends. Instead, you become adjusted to coping and aim to live the best life that you can with the skills that are available to you. This requires daily work and effort more than time.

Styles of Grieving

Some people will want to ask questions and look for answers following death and loss. They want to make sense out of something that may not really make sense at the time. For them it is important to assign meaning or responsibility for events that are completely out of their control. Grieving is about accepting that you have no control, and this may be why you may go through emotional stages of anger "I'll find out who's to blame," regret "I should have been here more often," and blame or guilt as you think, "It's all because of me. I'm to blame."

People also tend to focus on one of two aspects of grieving:

- **Instrumental Grieving**

This style of grief is focused on being busy and doing stuff so that you don't have to feel anything. Those who grieve in this way will tend to become absorbed in arranging things, and they will also be quick to return to work. They will not allow themselves to feel the emotions that the loss has caused, and conceivably, they will struggle with repressed emotions and grief at a later date. On the outside, you may seem to be coping really well while you are busy doing things; however, on the inside, you are probably struggling to come to terms with your loss and your sorrow.

- **Intuitive Grieving**

Emotions and how you react to them are at the forefront of this style of grieving. You want to share how you are feeling, talk about your experience with grief, and think about the way you feel about life and death. Sorrow becomes energy that moves you to look inward and express outward. Those following this style of grieving are likely to deal with their feelings well, however, they may struggle with entering the real world again and in making decisions and taking actions.

The best is to combine both styles of grieving to effectively process your emotions and maintain enough of a grasp on reality that you are able to function practically out in the world.

Finding Meaning

Sara loses her six-month-old baby boy to leukemia. She is absolutely torn and locks herself in her room for days on end. When she finally speaks to her husband, she tells him that she wants to start a charity that funds research into leukemia.

This example is a typical case of finding meaning in loss. In an almost religious sense, it is about making the death of someone you care about into a *good death*. It is about taking control, which is better than feeling out of control for most people. We are programmed by society to think that as long as something has meaning, it is okay. We believe that no one should die in vain. Yet, this belief does not lessen our pain or the sorrow that we experience with the loss of a loved one.

Wanting to find meaning may also be another delay tactic to avoid feeling the painful emotions that we deny inside ourselves.

Chapter 5:

Dealing with Others and Their

Expectations

When someone dies, we always feel the urge to comfort those who are grieving. It is an inborn human instinct to comfort others, to show our empathy and our sympathy. Yet, our comfort is not always expressed in a way that brings them any solace. Kind words that are meant to soothe someone may end up haunting them and bring them even greater pain and conflict.

While you are grieving, you are barely hanging on to your life, which seems to be completely out of control and broken. Having to deal with someone's offerings of advice and sympathy may not be something that you are up to in the moment that you see them. Instead, you may be in the anger stage of the Kubler-Ross theory, and you may just hate the world that took your loved one from you. In this state of mind, you may not be able to speak calmly to someone whose insensitive words might just light your fuse. So, what do you do then?

Dealing with people and their expectations of you when you are grieving is a tricky and often painful situation. You may justifiably want to tell them off. Being a little prepared can help you to avoid the most common of these painful scenarios; however, they are not fully avoidable. You may feel like you want to curl into a ball of self-pity and pain and never face the world again. The reality is that though your world may have stopped with the loss that you have suffered, the world out there continues spinning.

You will need to eventually rejoin the living. This may sound harsh, but it is a reality. To continue living, you need to go back to work, socialize again, spend time with your family, and you will need the friends who may at this point be annoying you to tears. Words you say now can cause you endless grief later, so being mindful not to burn bridges with people while you are absorbed in the pain of grieving is a wise course of action. After all, they mean well.

They Mean Well

When you are dealing with the rawness of grief, you may not be in the best frame of mind to listen to what other people are saying to you. They mean well. They will say things that may seem insensitive to you, things that may upset you, and even things that are wildly inappropriate. It is important to know that unless you are fortunate enough to be friends with a bevy of psychologists, the people around you will probably not know how to deal with the loss that you are facing either.

None of us are born with a guide on how to support people who are grieving. And even if they had read such a book, they might still end up missing the mark with their expressions of condolences or well-meaning advice. After all, none of us grieve the same, so how could there be a guide with the perfect thing to say to you. So, don't expect people to know just what to say.

Likewise, you may not know what to reply to the flood of condolences that you are being faced with. Thanking people for their words and thoughts can only go so far, especially when you are trying to deal with this massive disruption in your life. You probably don't fully understand what you are going to go through yet, and neither will your friends or family.

During the start of your grieving process, you may be feeling overwhelmed and confused, and it is natural to want to withdraw from the world so that you can begin reflecting and turn your focus inward to find your own way through your grief. At this time, you are not ready to face comments or expressions of support, regardless of how well-meaning they are. It is okay to feel this way. Don't be too hard on yourself for feeling like you want to withdraw. So, how can you respond without hurting a well-meaning friend or relative?

How to Handle Social Interactions After the Death of a Loved One

Social interactions are perhaps some of the worst aspects of grieving you will need to face after losing someone. While you may want to self-isolate so you can begin to grieve, you may also require some social support. Certainly, there are benefits to both approaches, and it does not have to be an either-or situation. You can benefit from both elements in combining time for solitude with having enough social support to keep you anchored to your life.

Once the grieving process starts, you may find that your interactions with people, the roles that you play and the roles that they play become redefined. These new roles may become expressed socially, and if you are not alerted to these changing dynamics, you may become defensive and hurt someone who is trying to express their condolences to you. Likewise, you may also express the need for someone to respect your privacy, refuse to answer intrusive questions, or even refuse to talk to someone you don't feel comfortable opening up to yet.

You may want to tell people to just leave you alone once you are starting to grieve, but you will need them later. So finding a non-offensive way to ask for space and time to begin grieving could become an essential skill. The difficulty is that every time someone tells you how sorry they are for your loss, it may mean that you feel that loss anew. Like people walk past and twist at the knife sticking into your heart. In a sense, it also means that those fragile scabs on the wound to your heart don't have time to form since they get scratched off the whole time by well-wishers.

This will be a period of adjustment to you, and you are well within your rights to limit your social circles to only include individuals who you feel are supportive and helpful to your grieving process. It is also okay to avoid entering into discussions about the death and your grieving with people who you don't feel comfortable with. You can even decide to not answer your phone for a while or to respond via text messages if you feel that phone calls are too much pressure. You need to find what works for you during this time, though it is essential to balance some isolation with limited and constructive social interactions.

These are some tips to help you navigate those fragile first few weeks:

- **Preplan Your Responses**

Your brain is running in overdrive when you are dealing with grief. When you feel pressured by people offering their "deepest condolences," you may end up answering in a way that may seem ungracious, or accidentally hurting feelings. The thing you may not realize at this point is that those people also don't really know what the right thing to say is. This is why many people rely on cards or quotes to express their sorrow towards you. Probably the worst is when they say, "Is there anything I can do for you?" This well-meaning offer sticks in your throat. Obviously, you would want them to return the person who you have lost. But no one can do that.

Having a pre-planned response will help you to deal with that awkward sensation of not knowing what to say. It doesn't need to show how unspeakably brave you are. It just needs to acknowledge that the other person is trying to be supportive, even if what they said was not helpful.

For standard condolences, you might respond with a basic reply such as, "Thanks for caring" or "I appreciate your kindness." Don't feel pressured to expand in this unless you feel up to it. People who prod a little by asking how you are doing require a little bit more delicacy in your response. You might answer them by saying, "It's all still very new to me, but I am learning to cope." Try to avoid saying things like, "I am okay." It may seem like the best way to get people off your back. It isn't. You are not okay, and no one expects you to be okay. People who offer their help can be answered by saying, "Thank you for the offer, I will let you know if I need anything."

However, you also need to prepare responses when you feel someone has said something that requires you to ask them to back off. Even though you may be raging on the inside, you certainly don't need to add to your woes by overreacting and then later feeling guilty at being abrupt with someone who you might still need in your life. In this case, you are not overstepping if you tell someone politely that you are still finding your way, and you will grieve in your own way and in your own time.

It may really boil your noodle to hear someone say, "When my husband died, I did (followed by some unhelpful advice)." Staying as calm as you can, you could reply with, "I understand that, and thank you for offering advice; however, I am finding my own way through this difficult time."

If they continue pushing, you are well within your personal rights to warn them off gently by adding, "Please respect my need for space and time for a while."

- **Prepare Evasions**

People may not understand your need to focus inward and self-isolate for a while. Being naturally concerned, they may want you to continue with your normal social activities such as going to book clubs and attending weekend picnics. They may even want you to join them more often since you now have so much "extra time without the person who died." This can be very hurtful to you; however, it is again their expression of concern, and you shouldn't take it as meaning disrespect to you or to the person who died.

Planning an escape route can be really helpful to guide you away from unwanted social activities. People are concerned that you aren't living outwards anymore, so by joining activities such as grieving support groups and perhaps taking up a new hobby, you will be able to convince them that you are living a balanced life. You do not have to accept their offers to go out simply to please them. It is okay to avoid some of the usual places that may remind you of the person who you lost.

Having responses prepared such as "I am trying some new things for a while" or "I am attending a support group, so please give me some time to adjust" are quite acceptable routes of escape from enforced social gatherings that you may not feel comfortable with.

- **Don't Take It to Heart**

People don't know how to deal with grief. Not their own grief and not someone else's grief. Only trained bereavement counselors may have answers and responses that could help you. Friends and family members are trying to do and say the best things they can. If their words hurt you, don't take it to heart.

Be careful of not turning the anger that you are feeling while you grieve on a well-meaning friend who says the wrong thing. Don't hold a grudge against them. They will probably feel terrible when they blurt out something that is insensitive to your grief. Don't be surprised that people may start to avoid you once you have begun grieving. This is because they may not know what to say, or how to respond. Be careful not to read these people as being insensitive or callous. They do care about you, but they struggle with articulating their care.

- **Expect Clumsiness**

You may even find that some of your friends will struggle with finding something to say, which could result in excessive hugs and deliveries of cooked meals as an expression of their condolences to you. When you do see them, they may feel awkward whenever you mention the person who died, and they may also react with confusion when they mention that person to you. Just as you are grieving the loss, they are probably also finding a way to move forward in how to communicate with you.

Be kind and show understanding of how they are feeling. If it continues, you might want to have a word with them, reminding them that you still care about them and that it is not their fault that your loved one died. If they admit to not knowing what to do, assure them that you understand (even if you feel like you don't) and simply ask them to be there for you when you ask. Try to avoid using emotionally-laden language as this will only worsen the situation. Remember that this is a friend or colleague who you are talking to. They are not the enemy.

- **Forgive Easily**

Grief often comes with resentment, and you may resent family members for not being there for you and the person who died (especially if that person was sick before their death). With all the negative emotions that you may experience during the initial stages of grief, it can be easy to hold a grudge against people who you feel failed you. Perhaps you should consider that this feeling might be about your grief and have very little to do with those people.

Forgiving easily is a way to ensure that you can move forward without creating further problems that you will need to deal with later. It will also help you to control some of the rage and anger that may be boiling up inside you.

- **Ask for Forgiveness**

While you may be able to forgive others when they say something that upsets your grieving process, you may struggle to ask others for their forgiveness. When we are grieving, we can often become so self-absorbed that we forget to consider other people and their grief. In the midst of our own pain and anguish at dealing with our loss, we may forget that we can also hurt someone else.

Asking for forgiveness is about being able to express your pain outwards, remain filled with empathy, and include others in what you are going through. It is never a weakness to apologize when you have spoken from a place of pain. Those you have hurt can still open up to you when you candidly open up to them and genuinely apologize. While knowing that you have hurt someone, the apology could form the basis of a greater friendship and relationship.

Family Dynamics After Death

When a family grieves after the loss of a family member, it can be an incredibly traumatic event. Though they grieve for the same person, they each grieve in their own way (Moorhead, 2017). These different forms of grieving can also lead to the family dynamics being redefined after death. This can be a traumatic process that may take some time to settle. You may even find that your family seems to fight more often as each family member has their own idea of how to go about the grieving process or how to make the arrangements. Then there are often the inevitable issues with the division of the deceased's assets and belongings, which can also cause horrific conflicts. It is important to remember that this is not about winning or getting out on top. Rather, it is about reaching a decision or agreement that will preserve as much of the family unity and your sanity as possible. This will require some negotiation from all parties involved, and you may end up actually needing an outside mediator to help resolve conflicts if necessary.

The dynamics of the family has been changed, and there is no going back. Where your father may have been there to support and advise you during your life, you may now be missing that figure in your life upon his death. If you were married and lost your spouse, you have suddenly become single again. If you lose your only child, you will become childless. All of these changes may not really be something that will initially hit you. Over time, you will realize how the death has changed you and your family.

While you may not know what the exact format of your family will become after losing a family member, you still need to build, preserve, and redefine your family's structure and bonds. There are a few aspects to be mindful of in making sure that you don't lose more than the deceased family member.

- ## Maintain Focus on Your Present Family Members

Loss is an overwhelming life event, and it may completely alter your and your family's focus. It is important to maintain your focus on your family members, assigning value, and sensitivity to them. Even though you may want to grieve completely on your own, you still need to acknowledge that you are part of a family. Your grief will affect others, but your grief can't be denied either. Try to avoid isolating yourself or hiding how you feel from your family members. This will not help you in the long run.

- ## Balance the Living and the Dead

Your family members who are still living should enjoy as much focus and energy as those family members who are no longer present. This means that you should not refrain from talking about the deceased at all. By talking about our loved ones who have died, we can help the grieving process along and ensure that we don't forget them. However, our lives can't begin to revolve around a person who is no longer there. Examples of this would be a woman who refuses to date again since she still sees herself as being in a relationship with her dead husband.

Though grieving is a natural part of life, you can't invest all of your energies in it. There should be a healthy balance between the living and the dead.

- ## Listen to Feelings Not Words

Not all of us are born with the natural ability to express how we are feeling when we are feeling it. In the heat of the moment, we may say the wrong thing. Being gifted with the skill to effectively articulate our emotions is not something we all enjoy. This means that we need to listen to what we can see someone is feeling, not necessarily what they are saying. A family member who says something like, "You are taking over the funeral arrangements" may actually feel that they are not given a chance to participate or that they are worried about you taking on too much.

Reading people's feelings can be difficult, but if you try to see what their expressions and behavior is telling you, then you will have a chance to really understand what they are trying to say. It is important that as your family dynamic changes, you listen to what each family member is saying *and* feeling. Don't make assumptions.

- **Establish Closeness**

During grieving, families need each member of the family. No single family member can be said to grieve more than the others. Instead, grieving is an opportunity for growing closer together and becoming more invested in each other's lives. Distant family members may reach out, seeking to establish closeness.

This is an opportunity to restructure and repair the family bonds that may have been neglected in the past. Making use of rituals and annual events such as celebrating birthdays, or having holiday parties may be a great way to form bonds and grow closer. This will also lead to families expanding and changing. While dad used to be in charge of carving the turkey every Thanksgiving, this can now be done by the oldest son (who shoulders some of the fatherly responsibilities in the family).

Using the re-allocation of roles can be a great way to bring the family closer together and help each other grieve.

- **Discuss Roles After the Loss**

Communication following the loss of a family member is essential. It may take some time to open channels of communication though. Don't fall into the trap of making assumptions. Just because Bob is the oldest son, does not mean that he will take the lead role in the family, or that he should plan the funeral alone. His younger brother, David, may be more suited to making the arrangements (or even Lisa, their sister).

Making assumptions about who should do what can create lasting resentments in the family about who gets to play what role. Open discussions with decisions made through consensus will help to smooth the way forward.

Going Back to Work

It is always a good idea to take some time off from work to tend to the funeral arrangements and other details that come with someone passing away. If you have never had to deal with this, you may be surprised by the overwhelming amount of details and planning that goes into it. To try and balance this with still working is not wise: apart from the obvious stress and strain that this will cause you, it is most likely that you will be distracted and preoccupied with the sheer burden of legalities, family considerations, and arrangements. You will not be able to focus on your work, though you may want to flee there since it represents some normalcy.

However, after a while, reality will come knocking, and you will have to return to work. You may think that this is a good thing, and perhaps it is. It represents life before your loss, and you will want to simply dive into the routines and activities that made sense to you before you lost that person who was so pivotal in your life. You may quickly discover that returning to work can also present its own challenges and some planning and strategies may help you transition more easily.

- **Don't Assume They Know**

Lisa returned to work a few days after the death of her husband. While in the break room, John, who had been on leave for a week, walked up to her with a large smile, asking when she and her husband were going to join his family for a weekend hike again.

The above scenario is everyone's worst nightmare. Lisa is justified in feeling upset that John isn't aware of her loss, while John is also not to blame for not knowing. While you may feel like the whole world should know you are grieving, there are probably a bunch of people who don't even have a clue. Your world stopped, theirs didn't.

It is important that you ensure the people you deal with regularly are aware that you are grieving. You may feel like the obvious dark cloud above your head is a clear sign that something is up, but people will not know what is going on until you tell them. This may be one of the reasons why people place an obituary in local newspapers. Apart from the legal ramifications, it also helps to inform people without having to actually go into all the details regarding your loss. Today, thanks to social media, it is easy enough to simply send out a message, post it on your Facebook wall, or inform people through Messenger or WhatsApp. This allows you to inform people without having to talk to each person, answer questions that you are not necessarily ready for, and avoid that awkward situation where you have to tell someone after they said something insensitive. You can even ask a friend or coworker to inform people on your behalf if you are still learning to cope. This would also help people understand that you need some space.

- **Get Busy**

Your mind may be filled with thoughts and plans associated with your loss. These distractions can be really traumatic to cope with, so it may be helpful to dive in and get busy with tasks at work. Filling your mind with the details of projects you are dealing with or people you need to interview can become a kind of meditation that will open your mind, letting some of the pain drain. The mundane aspects of your work can help you to focus on the now, and set your grief aside for just a little while. Remember that perspective is also a great healer.

- **Schedule Your Grief**

This may seem incredibly callous, but it is also practical. While you are at work, set aside time for you to admit to yourself (and others) that you are grieving. If colleagues keep asking you how you are doing, you may need to ask them to keep those questions for your lunch break or to talk to you after hours since you are focusing on your work. The upside of scheduling grief is that you don't avoid it entirely. Some people make the mistake of trying to deny their grief. Rather give yourself some time to hide away in your car during your lunch hour or go to a nearby park where you can sit quietly with a photo album or your husband's iPod and listen to their favorite tunes, remembering and grieving. Grief sometimes works better in increments. This will also help you avoid having melt-downs at work.

- **Accept Help**

If you are an independent person, you may struggle with this concept, but it will really help you in dealing with grieving and returning to work. Your colleagues may offer to help you ease back into work. Though you may want to decline this and muscle through your load, you would not be seen as being any less in accepting offers of help. This is not to say that you are unable to cope, but accepting help will also let you feel a sense of belonging and having someone care about you. It fosters a sense of community with your coworkers.

Should you accept help, feel free to ask for specific forms of help. This should be empowering to you, not a disempowering case of a colleague taking work from you since they think you aren't coping. Speak freely to anyone who offers to help, asking for specific help, or politely decline their offers if these are overbearing. You are in control (even if you don't feel like it).

- **You May Struggle to Focus**

Something that may really stick in your throat initially upon returning to work is that you could struggle to focus on your work, and obviously this may influence the quality of your work. You are still dealing with your grief, and you could be distracted. If you fear this will negatively influence your work, especially when you are in essential services, you might ask a coworker or supervisor to do a few double checks for you. This is about being responsible and not creating further problems down the line for yourself.

It is really important that you don't blame yourself for mistakes, though you should have a support network or check when you are doing work that affects lives. Accept that you may make mistakes and forgive yourself.

If your company has a large workforce, then they probably have a substantial HR department, which can be really helpful in dealing with your reintroduction to work. They might offer you benefits such as having a few half days available or arranging for extra leave to deal with some of the legal issues that come after the funeral. Some companies also offer counseling services to help employees who are grieving.

Building a Support Network

Grief makes you feel alone, and initially, you may seek this feeling out. You are still figuring out what your grief feels like, and you may not want other people around who try to help or counsel you. There is nothing wrong with this. However, you are not living in isolation. You share your grief with your family, friends, colleagues, and even members of your community.

At some point, you will need to function in a support network, and these people can help you to process your grief, move forward, let go of the pain while holding on to the memories. When considering your support network, there are some things to keep in mind and explore.

- **It's Your Choice**

You have the final say on who gets to be in your support network. If you feel uncomfortable around someone or feel that they are not helping you, it is up to you to exclude them from your social interactions. If you should feel that your friends aren't supportive or understanding enough, you may find yourself looking outward for others who do meet the need for acceptance and support that you may feel. You may find this change in social circles is especially evident if you are relatively new to grief and loss. Sadly, you may discover that some of your previous friends were fairweather friends, and this is not their or your fault. Nothing forces you to turn to friends who simply can't support you, and nothing prevents you from making new friends who are able to help you.

- **They May Also Be Grieving**

Due to the isolating nature of grief, you may find your attention being focused on your feelings and grief; however, your friends and family are also grieving for the loss of the person who died. Everyone grieves differently. While some of your friends or relatives may be goal-oriented towards dealing with moving on, others may choose to spend time reflecting on the person's life or their memories of them. There is no wrong or right way to grieve. While moving within your social circles, you need to be aware and respectful of this. Likewise, you need to get the respect for your path through grief from the people you associate with.

- **Plan for Bad Days**

Accept that your grieving may take a longer time than you anticipate. It could take months and even years to adjust to living with the sorrow of losing someone. There will be good days when you function fine, and there will be days when you don't want to go on at all. Plan ahead for both kinds of days. Have a group of friends who can support you when you are happy, who will not remind you of the pain that you managed to avoid for a day (or even a moment). Make sure you also have a group of friends or colleagues who can support you when you hit bottom. These should be people who will be sensitive enough to listen, be there, comfort, and accept your full grief flowing. Even if they only jump into bed next to you to keep you company while you cry into your pillow for hours, their presence and assurance that you are not alone will be enough.

- **There's No Shame in Getting Help**

If your current social circles are not meeting your changing needs during this time of grief, you can reach outside for help. This could take the form of bereavement groups or counseling; however, it can also take the form of new social groups like hobby groups or community groups. You may need the support of having someone around you who does not know that you are grieving and will just spend time with you as a form of release. There is nothing wrong with your own life also carrying on while you process your grief. Your life didn't stop.

- **Someone to Talk to**

In the end, we all need someone who we can talk to. We need that special person who we can vent to, form theories with, and speak plainly to–a soundboard. With the people who know us, we may feel restricted from voicing our real feelings, and we probably don't want to say something that may upset them. If your father passed away, you will probably not want to tell your mother that you still feel some anger towards him and perhaps upset her.

If this is the case, it may be better for you to find an objective outside party who you can confide in. A counselor or support group may be ideal in this regard; however, you can also use many online support groups that specialize in bereavement and grief counseling. The benefit here is that you can voice your feelings anonymously, and no one will judge you for what you say or feel. These are three excellent online groups that you may consider joining in building your support network:

Grieving.com

This online forum allows people to discuss their different experiences with grief based on a variety of topics. It may be helpful to read the experiences of other people who are grieving, to know that you are not alone, and to discover how different people approach and heal through grieving.

Recover-from-grief.com

This website has a range of resources as well as an online grief club that supports and helps people discover and deal with their grief. There are different areas of grief to consider communicating such as the loss of a parent, the loss of a child, and even the loss of a pet.

Thegrieftoolbox.com

This site offers a range of tools for those dealing with grief. Useful information, as well as an online platform to express your grief artistically, combined with a support group locator for the U.S. and the

U.K. combine to make this a very useful and motivating site to visit when building your support network.

When joining an online support group or forum, there are some basic rules to bear in mind. These rules are there to keep you safe and ensure that you don't fall prey to scams that target those who are vulnerable due to their grief.

Always keep your identity confidential. Don't give out your real information or where you live. Be careful of sites that ask for a joining fee, though many do so. Check if they accept payment through reputable sources and that your financial details are secure. Be careful about meeting someone in person who you have met in an online support group. Always remember that they are still a stranger to you, though you may have shared much of your most painful experiences with them online. Safety comes first, so if you decide to meet in person, do so in a public place and make sure that someone you know goes with you or knows where you are.

People have different expectations of what it means to grieve, but it is a personal process and none of us grieve in the same way. There is no right or wrong way to grieve, but it is wrong to impose our expectations of grief on others. Grieving is about healing yourself after suffering a loss. You may start doing so alone, but you will have to continue living in the real world with real people, many of whom will want to help you. If, how, when, and from who you accept help is up to you. A support network can help you through difficult times when you don't know if you can carry on. It can help you find your voice and make sense of what you are feeling. An effective support network can also be a life-line if you find your grief spiraling out of control.

Chapter 6:

When Grief Lasts Longer Than

You Think Possible

Nobody can tell you how long you should mourn for; however, grief is supposed to fade into a bearable sorrow that still hurts, but that you can handle. When grief starts to interfere with the quality of your life, steals your joy, and darkens your life in the long term, then you are dealing with the debilitating effects of complicated or complex grief.

It is quite normal to feel this way within the first couple of weeks or even a month or two after losing someone who you loved. Coping with your grief does not lessen it, but you are supposed to compartmentalize and organize your grief (even if that sounds unfeeling). If you were to think of grief as a disability, the body would learn to cope with the loss of a limb, even though you might end up limping for the rest of your life. Grief that stops you in your tracks and limits your life and the business of living is something that needs interventions.

Complicated Grief and Being Stuck

It is fallacious thinking to believe that your grief will magically vanish within a certain amount of time. In fact, you may never get over your grieving at all. There is nothing wrong with feeling sad 15 years down the line when you think about the person you lost. However, breaking down and feeling hysterical or stopping your own life a year after the person died is not natural or good for you. This might mean that you are stuck in the grieving process.

Grief is supposed to evolve in response to your mourning process. It is supposed to settle and soften, becoming a dull ache that is there but does not limit your life. When grief follows this pattern, you can be assured that you have processed your grief and integrated it in a meaningful and practical way into your life.

If your grief remains raw, with no signs of it lessening or settling, then you are perhaps dealing with complicated grief. There are four unique aspects to complicated grief that help to identify and understand what brings about this form of grief and how to treat it. However, according to the Mayo Clinic, there is no hard and fast rule for when grief devolves into complicated grief. It is suggested by research that only 15% of those who grieve will experience complicated grief. The four aspects have much in common with the Kubler-Ross stages; however, the last aspect is unique in applying to complicated grief.

- ### Disbelief

It is quite normal to experience some disbelief when you lose someone. For many, viewing the body before the funeral is helpful in this regard as it solidifies the loss, allowing the brain to accept the fact that the person is indeed no longer alive. There may even be some biological basis for this since even animals follow this method of accepting death.

In the wild, animals will often linger with the body of one of the herd before moving on. Farmers will often let a foal or calf stay with the mother that died for an hour or more to lessen the amount of grief calling that the young will make. If the offspring do not realize that their mother is dead, they will keep crying for her, believing that she has been moved somewhere else.

However, with humans, this can become complicated when there are no remains or the death was so traumatic and disfiguring that it is not possible to view the body. Many relatives have admitted that the death only became real once they saw their beloved's body.

- ### Anger and Bitterness

This is not an easy aspect of grief to deal with. You may become angry at the person who died, blaming them for dying or others for causing their death. Bitterness can set in, causing a flood of negative emotions. However, this is still normal if you can move on to the next stages of grief, processing the loss, and carrying on with life and living.

In those experiencing complicated grief, this stage becomes enmeshed with the following stages, and anger remains within them, poisoning their lives and world view.

- ### Painful Emotional Yearning and Longing

When grief evolves into sorrow, it is progressing along the natural acceptance and mourning process that we all experience after losing someone we love. With complicated grief, these feelings can stagnate, and your longing and yearning can begin to dominate your feelings and ruin your ability to move on with life. It becomes a case of wallowing in misery (harsh as this may sound). Those suffering from complicated grief are unable to move past their pain and the longing they feel, regardless of how much time has passed.

- ### Preoccupation and Intrusive Thoughts

Finally, with complicated grief, you are constantly thinking of the person you lost. It may even express itself as an inability to function normally in your life. You are constantly distracted and struggle to experience other normal emotions such as joy or excitement in your normal interactions. In worst cases, you may not even know who you are without that grief. You become consumed by your grief, becoming a victim of your loss, and your identity becomes defined as being a widower/widow or someone who lost a child or family member. Over time, you will no longer have any interest in living or participating in life. This may in rare cases present itself in forms of suicidal thinking, as some people may even want to join the person they lost in death.

Complicated grief is often most seen when you have never lost someone before and lack the skills to deal with death and grieving, or when you have a preexisting mental condition such as depression that limits your ability to cope. Not having a support base can also lead to complicated grief as you may be trying to deal with your grief alone, which can lead to a warped sense of reality.

There are many views on how long someone needs to be suffering through grief before it can be defined as complicated grief, but once it negatively affects your ability to continue living productively and begins to negatively affect your thinking patterns, it is a safe bet that you are struggling to process your grief.

Dealing With Complicated Grief

In dealing with your grief, it is better to judge the success of your own coping process by looking at how you are feeling as a whole, not at how long you have been grieving. Some people need more time to mourn, and though they may take longer to process their grief, they do make steady upwards progress. Other people struggle and feel completely overwhelmed by their grief. If you fall into this last group, you may need to seek professional help and counseling. Even when you are making some progress, but still feel overwhelmed at times, you may benefit from seeking professional help. After all, we are only as capable as the resources available to us. Grieving is a skill that we develop based on our resources and experience.

Even if you approach a therapist, and they only confirm that you have been coping well or that you are entitled to feel sad and low, that is also useful. Seeing a therapist may help you identify that you are struggling with an adjustment disorder, which can happen whenever you are facing a major life change that is causing you stress. Feeling stressed is not necessarily a bad sign; in fact, it would be abnormal for you to feel nothing when dealing with grief.

There are many different forms of therapy for complicated grief, each focusing on different aspects of it, depending on how this grief presents in your life. If you have difficulty remembering the person who you lost without breaking down, you may avoid thinking about that person, or even avoid the places or aspects of your life that have something to do with them. This is unnatural since the person was a part of your life and denying them, in the long run, is like cutting away a part of your life. In this case, therapy may involve loss focused activities. You would be encouraged to remember the person, not just their death, but also their life in narrative-based activities where you tell their (and your) story. Journaling, writing, and celebrating positive events of your life with them would fall within this type of counseling.

Therapies for complicated grief often focus on helping you to discover who you are without the person you were dependent on who died. Such therapies are about helping you see yourself as being independent of the grief and focus forward instead of being consumed by the loss, which is in the past. In some cases, it may be necessary to combine this with medication such as antidepressants. This may help to regulate some emotions that have become destructive until you are able to cope better. Deciding to use medication to help you deal with grief is not a decision to take lightly, though.

Complicated grief is different from normal grief which settles and runs its course, becoming a part of your life without defining your life. When you process your grief and begin mourning, you are able to live forward, instead of only thinking backward. If you are struggling to cope with this process, you may need to find outside help to guide you through the unfamiliar terrain of grief integration.

Getting Help

Knowing when to get help, or when to ask for help is a difficult concept for many of us. If you fear to admit that you are not coping and that you need help, you are not alone in this. Getting help from a professional can be a life-line when you are at the end of your rope. Whether you are suffering from complicated grief or not, you might simply need the knowledge and skills to better deal with your grief.

Admitting that you need help is not a weakness. It isn't a sign that you are a failure. Instead, it means that you are human, and you aren't doing okay right now. However, with therapy and counseling, you could be doing much better soon.

During counseling or therapy, a trained professional will help you to discover, express, and process your feelings. This will start the process of acceptance and forming a new life view. Your pain will never disappear; thinking like that is an example of magical thinking (it will never happen). Therapy helps you to understand your grief, make peace with it, lessen it, and interpret it in ways that have meaning to your life.

By engaging with your loss through focused activities and exploring the depth and range of your experience, you can begin to see events and your future in a new light. If your pain was so raw that you could not even speak about the person who died, you may benefit from narrative therapies where you discover how to acknowledge and speak about the person you lost.

Through therapy, you will be able to understand that your grief does not only affect yourself. Even though you may be suppressing your pain at the moment to spare your family, you may be doing them an even greater injustice by not grieving fully. If you have lost a child, your inability to process their passing may affect your other children or your spouse in ways that you don't yet fully understand or even see. Therapy can help you to realize this and bring closure to yourself and your family.

While your grief becomes integrated into your life through the process of mourning, you may discover that your grief can become renewed by events or situations that trigger your pain anew. Therapy can help you to do some personal maintenance of your coping mechanisms when your grief resurfaces and pressures your abilities.

Grief changes you. There is no way to return to who you were before your grief. This does not mean that you or your life has ended. Instead, you have changed, and with therapy, you can decide whether that change is for the better or worse.

While wanting or needing to get help, you could also guide those who are trying to help you. This is not easy for them either, and they may each have an idea of how they can best help you. Your family and friends, though not professional counselors, are certainly willing and committed to helping you during this difficult progression of your life. Psychotherapist Julia Samuel has written extensively about how to help someone who is grieving (Moorhead, 2017). The following are some helpful techniques that you could use to support others who are grieving, or use to guide your own support network in how to help you:

- **Listen**

You do not have to say anything. No one expects you to say something that will be so profoundly moving and healing that the person who is grieving will magically be all better. Just listen. Let the person who is grieving talk. Let them vent, cry, rage, blame, and explode in whichever emotional way that they need. There is no need for you to comfort them in any way beyond your presence, which is enough support so that they do not feel alone. Remember that every time they can tell the story of their loss, or recall a memory of the person who they lost, they will feel just a little bit of their load drift away. Your ability to listen can lighten their burden more than you can ever know.

- **Focus on Their Need**

You may want to comfort, and you may want to help the person who is grieving. Accept that this is about them. It is not up to you to fix them. They had no control over death, and they certainly don't need you to take control away from them by forcing them to talk when they don't want to or visit when they want to be alone. Set aside what you want and simply let them lead you to what they want. Grief is about them. Make sure to leave the control of their grief in their hands. This can be incredibly difficult when you are a naturally caring person, and you may be tempted to try and take their grief. Accept that you can't; it's theirs.

- **Be There**

For many of us, it is awkward to be around someone who is grieving. Mourning is not pretty, and it certainly doesn't attract a fan club. People tend not to know what to say, and this leads to them avoiding someone who is grieving. You don't need to say much. The person who is grieving will probably not want a speech about how great the person who died was. They know this, and it isn't helpful while they are in pain. A simple offer to be there for them and a kind gesture is enough. Then check up on them later. Drop by their house and bring them some flowers or fresh veggies as they are probably not doing much shopping now. If they want to talk, then listen. If they want solitude, then leave. Don't take offense and don't avoid them.

Moving on after loss can be a scary proposition for many of us. Without this grief and pain, who are we? Living with a life moved by mourning means that we need to redefine what is normal for us. What rituals will we use to honor the life that was lost, instead of only remembering the death that happened? Normalcy is possible with consistent effort and greater insight. Now set your feet on the path before you; there is a way forward.

Chapter 7:

The Way Forward–Regaining a

Sense of Normalcy

As we live, you may discover that normal is a subjective concept. It is really just about what we are used to. With grief, we struggle to come to terms with the flood of unfamiliar emotions and thoughts that are prompted by someone we cared about passing. Finding normalcy is rather about creating a new state of mind and accepting your reality, improving what you can, and letting go of what you can't.

Moving forward, you can find a way to live happily after death, create your own life path that is not dictated by pain, and learn to make decisions again by acting and not reacting. You do not have to make living with pain and loss your new normal, and you don't have to become used to this stage of your life. You have the power to adapt and change. Take that power now and live.

Life After Death

There is life after death. No, this is not meant to reflect on some otherworldly experience that those who die go to. Rather, this is about you, those who remain here after someone has died. And, yes, there is life for you after your loved one has died. You may wonder if life will be business as usual. You may want things to just go back to the way they were before you suffered loss and pain; it won't.

It isn't as simple as that, though. Life will change, and nothing will be quite the same. But life will continue anew. And there is the crux of the matter. Life will be renewed. It will continue with changes, becoming a new and different life. It is simply different, made richer and more tender by the experience with loss and grief that you have worked (and continue to work) through.

Life will not return to normal as you knew it before you lost someone precious to you. Instead, life will be redefined, and you will create a new normal. Over time, the pain that you feel and the emptiness you hold in your life due to having lost someone dear will soften, and it will no longer dominate your life as much. You will laugh again, you will feel happy again, and you will live again. Time is a great healer, but you also need to play your part in creating a new normal and living your life to the full.

Making Your Own Blueprint

There's a popular saying, "Today is a gift, that's why it is called the present," which is attributed to a wide range of motivational speakers, and even Kung Fu Panda said it. It may sound like something out of a Hallmark card, but it is an irrefutable truth. You have lost someone, but they are no longer a part of this day. Someone you loved has shaped you for *your* future, and now you need to step forward. It is not about moving on, or letting go. You will always carry the memory of them, and you should cherish it. However, you should not let that memory hold you back. You have a wonderful gift in your hands: this moment (and the moments after this one).

Moving forward means taking control of your life and stepping into the driver's seat. You need to create your own designs for the future. You need to make up your own plans for your destiny. You are more than your grief.

The concept of creating your own life blueprint applies here. It is about deciding what stays, what goes, what you should explore, and what you should avoid. You can create routines and structures that help you shift gears and also build in soft places to crash when you feel like you are losing control.

You are adjusting, and no one has the right to push you when you are not ready. It is up to you to decide when you should return to work, though in reality, you may be financially forced to do so. This is one pressure that may work in your favor, though. While it may be good to take some time to deal with the overwhelming process of realizing and organizing your grief, you may also benefit from not having too much time on your hands. Returning to work may help you realize that you are not alone and that you have a support network that includes coworkers, friends, and family.

Being back at work can also help you break the inertia that sets in following a loss and the onset of grieving. However, you should be careful while creating your new life blueprint not to turn work into a hiding place from your grief. Work can help you find the determination to get up every day, to get dressed, to go out, to eat breakfast, and to pack lunch when you really don't want to do anything other than lie in bed all day. However, work is not your own personal cemetery where you go to die. You are still alive, and you should keep on living.

Finding new interests and hobbies will also help your blueprint form and shape your new life and living experience. Hobbies are great because they will help you to make decisions. Being able to make a decision, to choose between two or more options is a sign of being able to step forward. You need to decide whether you will eat take-out or cook a healthy meal for yourself now that you have been made single by losing a partner. Choosing to wear a new outfit and to smile is a better option than choosing to lounge around in your PJs all day, feeling sorry for yourself and not looking at what choices you still have.

These life choices are not easy. It would be so much easier to just curl into a ball and hide in a hole in the ground, instead of choosing to live, to face the heartache and sorrow that you feel each day, and to decide to move on even though you may feel like you can't.

Your blueprint can include healthy activities to help you cope with and adjust to having grief become an extra emotion in your life. You can't deny your sorrow since it won't go away, though, it will lessen with time and with care. This care is something that you should show yourself. Self-care activities like going to the hairdresser, or joining a gym after you return to work can help you to take care of yourself.

You may want to hold onto the memories that you have of the person you lost. Indeed, in some cultures, it is acceptable practice to build a shrine to the deceased. However, if you are going to commemorate their lives (which have ended), you should also celebrate your life (which is going on). This means that you should take photos of new events, challenges, hobbies, skills, and people in your life. Remember that you should balance the living and the dead. You can give yourself permission to be happy, to live, and to explore.

As part of your life blueprint, you should also include room for those who are still with you. If you look hard enough, you will find people who look up to you and depend on you. Even if you don't have children who need you, there are probably people in your life who don't want to lose you. Make space for these people. This means spending time with, talking to, and caring about the people in your life such as your friends, family members, colleagues, and even strangers who you meet and interact with every day. Giving love and expressing caring can be a great healing balm to your heart. When you feel needed, you will find more meaning and purpose in your life.

When you are ready to start building your life from this new blueprint, you may be reminded of the old adage, "Rome wasn't built in one day." Take small steps and be realistic. You can't wake up one morning and expect everything to be a hundred percent better. That would be setting yourself up for failure. Instead, you can lay the foundation over a period of several weeks or even months where you process your grief, find new resources for your process of mourning such as talking to friends, taking up new hobbies, and even attending counseling.

Once you feel more stable, you can start to reach out for the rest of the construction process, making new friends, finding *and* creating a more happy state of mind, and taking pride in the new life you have made for yourself. Setting yourself even just one goal a day can help you slowly build up your life anew. Take it slowly and pause when you need to rest or breathe. It is also okay to take some downtime when you need it. Even builders know that a foundation needs time to set before you can build further on it. Be kind to yourself and give yourself time when you need it, but keep the blueprint in mind.

As part of your blueprint, you will discover new things that are important to you. Remember that your life has changed, and your life is allowed to become different from what it was before. Take some time to decide what matters to you. While you are discovering new aspects of yourself, you may also redefine what makes you happy.

You probably won't be able to fill in the gap left in your life by your loss, but in discovering new things and finding things that please you and bring you joy, it is possible to lead a healthier life while you mourn. Eventually, you may even see that you can learn something from your loss and that it need not be only a negative force in your life.

Following your blueprint, you can take action, in small daily steps, to help you rebuild. Richard Ballo, a renowned author and speaker, suggests that it is possible to have happiness and health after going through loss (n.d). Techniques such as journaling, joining a support group, giving yourself enough time, reaching out through volunteer work, engaging in self-care activities, making new memories and traditions, and talking about and sharing memories of the person you lost can all help you to heal and become strong again.

Other aspects to add in your blueprint may include:

- **The Structure of Work**

Though you should not return to work before you are ready to do so, it can offer a type of therapy to you when adjusting to life with grief. When you are grieving, you are probably at an all-time low regarding your self-esteem. Having the structure of work can help you find stability and purpose to carry you through the toughest times of the mourning process. Work also offers some distractions that can help you bring your grief into perspective. Additionally, the work environment also helps you to mingle and break down the tendency to self-isolate when you are not doing well.

If you can restructure your life to include meaningful work where you can build yourself up, you will enjoy the benefits not only in your professional life but also in your grief work.

- **Be More Social**

Humans are herd creatures. We need to be around people. Yet, our grief can make us avoid people, and if this happens for long enough, we may no longer want to socialize or fail to realize that we need to do so. Your blueprint should include reaching out to people. If this does not come naturally to you, then you could plan certain days when you go out for drinks with friends, even if you don't really want to at that time. You may want to force yourself to say yes to social invitations. With this goes the reality that you can give yourself permission to have a good time. Your grief will still be there when you are ready to work on it some more.

- **Plan Control**

Death is the ultimate form of being left with no control whatsoever. Taking back control will empower you to be more positive and productive. Sorting through the deceased's belongings is one way of claiming control again. Stepping into your new roles and responsibilities will also help. A grieving husband may take up cooking lessons if his partner died. This kind of positive action is about regaining some control.

- **Action and Meaning**

Now that you are starting to regain some control over basic daily choices, you can begin to be more engaged in doing things. You may want to study something, take classes, join groups, learn about new things, and start looking after your health. Being active leads to forward energy, and you may naturally want to find some meaning to what happened to you. Finding healthy outlets for this search is a constructive addition to your blueprint.

- **Meals With Meaning**

Extending your actions to be more caring about your health, you can begin to pay special attention at mealtimes. It is also a great opportunity to invite someone around to nourish your need for social interactions. Making this a regular event can help structure your life, giving you something to look forward to and focus your attention on. Having Sunday lunch be a regular feature with some friends who come over will help you deal with the loneliness that comes with bereavement. Through the week, you can engage in a pleasant distraction of finding recipes to try, buying ingredients, and even shopping for something new to wear. All of these are positive actions that help to heal you and bring meaning to your life where you may have thought that death had robbed you of this.

- **Looking Forward**

With grief and mourning, you tend to look inward. This also means that you will be looking to the past, dwelling on your memories with the deceased. While you try to cope, you will probably be living from moment to moment and day to day. It can become really difficult to lift your eyes and look forward to tomorrow or next week. Planning is a great way to start living a little bit more forward. It doesn't have to be a giant leap into the future. Even planning where you will be buying your groceries tomorrow is a start. If you have taken up a hobby, you may start planning your next hobby project. If you are cooking for friends, you can plan who to invite and what you will make. This is also a great way to make and keep commitments, which may also have become difficult for you. When dealing with death, you may not want to make any commitments since you are overwhelmed with the transience of life. Yet, commitments are what keeps us going.

- **Express Yourself**

Being proactive with your emotions is a good way to survive your grief. In your blueprint, you should look for ways to express what you are feeling. The grief in you is like water entering a sinking boat, and you need to learn how to deal with it. You can scoop out water by writing, journaling, learning new things, and reading to fill your empty heart. All of these are techniques that help you empty out the excess pain, guilt, sorrow that forms in your lifeboat. Expressing yourself will also help you to eventually find the hole in your lifeboat and begin to repair it.

Grieving is not something that is done and dusted, and then you move on. It is something that requires maintenance or check-ins. This means that you need to include strategies to manage your emotions as they pop up in your blueprint for moving forward.

Your blueprint should include looking at your day in an objective way, analyzing every activity to decide whether it adds to or takes from your life and whether it is a positive experience or a negative echo of your loss. Plan things that fill your time and bring you happiness, and engage in tasks that help you cope. You can take charge, and you can find new direction.

Making Big Life Decisions

While you are rearranging your life and building your new path forward, you may be tempted to make big life decisions. We are drawn to drastic changes or dramatic examples. The truth is that you are grieving and mourning, which means that you are likely at the end of your rope already. You will not be in the best or most clear state of mind at this point, nor will you be physically at peak health. Now is not the time for massive life-altering decisions.

There are some life decisions that you should postpone for a while after losing someone. These decisions require you to be of a more logical and practical frame of mind, while grief is currently sending you through an emotional rollercoaster. Some decisions that you should not engage in at the moment (if you can avoid it at all) include:

- **Moving to a New Home**

If you have suffered a traumatic loss, you may struggle to live in the same house as you lived in with the person who died. This is most especially true when the loss happened in the home, such as having your spouse or child die at home. A place that was filled with memories and cherished moments will seem contaminated by tragedy and loss. However, you should not pack up and sell your house. It is still your home, and you need time to process what happened.

At the best of times, deciding to sell a house and move is a huge decision that requires months of planning. You should take some time to process your grief before you sell off a place that was part of your memories with the person you lost. Our memories are often grounded in places such as our homes, family vacation spots, and local parks. Selling your home could later feel like you sold those memories too.

Unfortunately, the option to keep your home may not be in your hands if your finances no longer allow for you to afford or keep the home. In the case of a parental home, you may be forced to say farewell to that space sooner in fulfillment of the final will and testament that may require the home to be sold so that funds can be divided.

If it is within your power to remain in your current home, you should do so until you are able to make a logical decision and leave the property without leaving the memories behind. It is advisable to try and keep the home for at least six months. This is often enough time to begin accepting some aspects of your grieving process.

- **Throwing Out Stuff**

As with making a rash decision to move, throwing out the mementos and belongings of the person who died should not be done in haste. You don't know what you will cherish most, or what sparks hope and joy in you. If you throw something out, it is gone forever. Given the fluidity of grief, you may find later that what seemed like an insignificant item can help you come to terms with your loss or serve as a reminder of what a pivotal person you have lost.

If the memories are too painful at this point, you can consider storing the deceased's possessions until you can handle looking through them and make better decisions on what to keep and what to let go. Time will give you some perspective on what is at the moment an emotional fire for you.

After taking some time, it is a natural process to let go. If you struggle with letting anything go, it may be a sign that you need professional help and counseling. Enshrining the deceased's life is not healthy for you, and it may end up only serving as a painful reminder of your loss. This can often be seen in parents who refuse to clear the room of a child who died. Keeping possessions as they are (refusing to move anything) is not healthy and will only prolong and worsen the grieving process, stopping you from mourning naturally.

- **New Jobs**

Grief is not pleasant. It hurts. It is a natural human instinct to want to start over and run away from what is hurting you. This may involve quitting your job and moving to a different city so that you can avoid seeing the places, people, and things that remind you of everything you have lost. After some time, you may benefit from a change; however, immediately after your loss, you should remain in your community and work environment. You have more than enough to deal with without causing an even bigger upheaval in your life by changing jobs.

Your work environment and community life form part of your support base. Your job offers you some familiar surroundings and structure that helps you to begin processing your emotions. Changing to a new job will bring the added tensions of unfamiliar surroundings and new people.

- **Finances**

Money is perhaps one of the worst aspects of grieving that people don't consider before losing someone. We each have roles in our relationships, and one partner is usually more dominant in making decisions. This means that loss can render one partner ill-prepared for making decisions about money and spending.

Scam artists enjoy targeting widows and widowers due to them being vulnerable. Therefore, it is more advisable to stop yourself from spending large sums of money following a loss. What you may think is a wise purchase now may turn out to be a money pit that will affect your future negatively.

- **Love**

In relationships, we all know about the concept of the rebound relationship, a relationship doomed to failure because it is engaged in for the wrong reasons. Losing someone is a painful experience, and you might crave a way to fill up the hole that death left in your heart. Looking for love could end in failure not because of the other person, but because of your inability to move forward.

It is wiser to refrain from engaging in relationships for a while after losing someone. This would wipe the slate of your heart a bit so that you can engage in a relationship with someone based on who they are and not on your need for them. Love requires equal footing. Don't enter into romantic relationships when you still have one foot firmly in the life of the person you lost. It is not fair to your new would-be partner, and it isn't fair to you either.

Give yourself time to heal and form a real emotional connection before starting up a romantic relationship. This will ensure that you can enjoy real happiness and contentment in your life ahead. Starting a relationship with a romantic partner within six months of losing your partner (or even your child) is not wise. Your emotional equilibrium needs time to recover, and your needs should not dictate your actions when you are vulnerable.

As a hard and fast rule, any major life decisions and choices should be put on hold for at least six months while you find your feet again following a loss and the process of bereavement. Your focus should be on yourself, the person who died, the people already in your life, and how to move forward. Jumping into decisions would be a disservice to yourself and those around you. Give yourself time, be patient in your choices, and plan the best path forward.

Learning Happiness After the Loss of a Loved One

When your grief is still raw, the thought of being happy again may seem foreign and even sinful. Chances are that you are toting around a bag filled with guilt along with regret. Once you engage with your grief, you may begin to unpack that bag and find your way forward towards happiness and joy.

Finding happiness after loss is a learning process. Just as you learned to grieve and how to make the sorrow a presence in your life that you can cope with and not lose to, you need to learn to be happy again. This may require some changes to your life view and acceptance that there is no overnight miracle cure.

In rediscovering your happiness, you may find the following considerations beneficial:

- **There Is Enough Time**

When you deal with death, you become aware of mortality–theirs and yours. Time ran out for the person you lost, but it has not run out for you. You may feel rushed. Don't. There is enough time to do all that you need to do. Instead of speeding through life, you can slow down, take your existence off autopilot and start seeing life for the wonder and beauty that is around you.

- **Let Go and Hold On**

Grieving and mourning is about letting go of the overwhelming emotions that weigh you down, holding on to the bitter (better) sweet memories and moving ahead, enriched by the life that was shared with you (even though you lost them). There may be days when you feel more sorrow than fondness and other days when you can smile and laugh at a beautiful memory with that special person who passed. With time, you will find a balance that makes your life more than bearable. You can remember and be happy and not just sad.

- **Lean On Them**

You are not alone in your grief. Even though you feel alone at times, and perhaps you even feel abandoned by the person who died, you are not alone. There are people in your life who care about you and want to help you. It is okay to lean on them, to accept a helping hand, or a kind word when you need solace. No one said you had to do this alone, so don't. Happiness will come through the comfort of a shared community. Even though your life's dynamics have changed, you are still loved and valued by those who are in your life and also by those who will come into your life in the future.

- **Move Small and Celebrate Big**

You don't need to make massive changes to your life after grief to be happy again. All you need to do is move forward one step at a time. It is important to value yourself for every effort that you make and to celebrate every positive step and accomplishment. You are rebuilding your life and should see each new addition as a resounding success. Whether it is making your first purchase after deciding on your own, choosing to join a social group, fixing a toilet without the man of the house (and of your life), or ironing your own pants before work–you are succeeding, so celebrate it. The little things can bring you joy when you least expect it.

- **Carry Them With You**

Death is such a poorly understood concept. It is not a solid wall or a permanent end. There is no reason why you can't carry the person you love with you after they pass away. You can cherish their memory, make new memories and still enjoy their presence in your life. It only becomes a problem when you can't live in the present because you live in the past. Processing your grief need not mean letting go of the person who died. Instead, you can redefine your relationship with them.

- **Create Memories**

Our lives are filled with traditions that we have. We make up rituals throughout our lives that add quality and connection to our existence. You may have had special habits and traditions with your loved one. Now that they are gone from your present, you can begin to create new traditions and habits. These should be celebrations of life and happy moments that you can create memories with going forward.

If you used to dance in the kitchen with your husband before he died, you might consider getting a dog that you can walk, or joining a dance class to form new memories and habits that can bring you joy.

- **Reconnect**

Our lives are busy. Unfortunately, there simply aren't enough hours in each day to reach out to everyone in our lives. The passing of one person may open up an opportunity for you to reconnect with someone who had been somewhat neglected in the past. You could find yourself striking up old friendships, forming new friendships, and meeting new people. Connecting and reconnecting is important as this will bring a sense of belonging back to your life, paving the way to contentment.

- **It's Okay to Not Be Okay**

Grief is circular, and you will have days when you aren't doing okay. Don't hide this and don't feel the need to avoid it or apologize for it. Feel what you feel completely. If you want to cry for your husband who died a year ago, then do so. Denying your feelings will only leave you feeling hollow. Instead, let yourself experience the full range of your emotions, making sure to feel the good and the bad. Over time, there will be more good than bad.

Conclusion

Grief is unavoidable. We will all of us in our lifetimes lose someone we love. Most often it will be a complete case of being blindsided by an unexpected loss. Sometimes we will have some forewarning as with someone who is terminally ill or frail; however, that will not make their passing any less traumatic or less painful. If anything, it might even be worse as there is then also the anticipation of grief and loss. Learning to cope with loss, manage your grief, and move forward with hope are skills that we can all benefit from acquiring. Sadly, we are usually ill-equipped to deal with death.

The Road of Grief

When you start down the path of grief, it is important to know that you don't walk it alone. The initial numbing shock of losing someone dear may be overwhelming and terrifying and confusing. Know that this is okay. It doesn't mean that you loved that person any less if you struggle to articulate your grief. We all grieve differently.

This book not only helped you to understand your own numbness and initial reactions to grief in chapter 1, it also busted some grief myths, helped you understand how grief and mourning are not the same and how to deal with sorrow in chapter 2.

Chapter 3 guided you through the most prominent theory surrounding grief with an overview of the Kubler-Ross stages of grief theory. Though your own unique grief may not follow this exact progression through grief, it is helpful to know that there are stages to grief.

Understanding that grief may cycle through the different stages before you reach the point of having adapted to grieving helps so that you are mourning and no longer suffering as deeply. Knowing that you may alternate between anger and depression even after you reached some level of understanding and that this is normal may help you to keep hope alive and continue healing day by day.

Your grief may not follow the stages theory at all, and this is also okay. None of us approach grief the same, and there is a range of other theories and beliefs around grief and the route to healing. Chapter 4 examined some other dominant theories and ideas about grieving, and many of these may have helped you to understand your own process better.

Grief is an individual process, but it involves others. Your family, friends, community, and coworkers all partake in the process, whether you want them to or not. Chapter 5 equipped you with some strategies for dealing with returning to work, moving in your social circles, dealing with questions, and managing your answers. It is important to have a support network, and there are people who you will want to include as well as people who you will want to avoid for this. Having discovered the techniques and methods for choosing and building your support network, you will have encouragement, understanding, and help not just for your healing period but also for the life that comes after your grief fades.

When you can't move on and struggle every day to set one foot in front of the other no matter how long it has been after the loss, the chances are that you are suffering from complicated grief. Chapter 6 guided you through the difficult road of counseling, professional interventions, and medication that may help you to find your feet and move along the grieving process.

Finally, chapter 7 helped you face what comes after death and loss—life. Planning your life with a heart that has grown through and survived loss is a process that you should not neglect. Normal has changed, and so should you. From building your own life blueprint to dealing with big life decisions, you are now able to find happiness one day at a time, one step at a time, and one moment at a time.

A Last Word

"Grief can be the garden of compassion. If you keep your heart open through everything, your pain can become your greatest ally in your life's search for love and wisdom." Rumi (Persian poet and scholar).

No one wants to grieve. It isn't pleasant to be so soaked in sorrow and pain that your whole world wants to crash down. But there is a bright side to it, even though it seems impossible for there to be anything good that can come from grieving. Yet, in the words of Rumi, we learn that in grieving we find compassion not only for ourselves but also for others. On the other side of grief is wisdom and love made all the deeper by the suffering that you have tasted and survived.

Keep your heart open, despite the despair and pain that you feel. Let the emotions wash through you as you become stronger and wiser, being able to help those who come after you on the path of bereavement.

Thank you for walking this road through your grief and choosing this book to help you walk each mile to personal growth and the rediscovery of happiness. If this book has helped you to know more about grief and how you are responding to it, we encourage you to share it by writing a favorable review on Amazon.com.

Remember, you can control and overcome your grief, making it into an ally to remind you of the one you lost, instead of being brought low by your sorrow. Happiness is within your reach, don't lose hope.

References

Clark, J. (2020). The Five Stages of Grief: Learning About Emotions After Loss Can Help Us Heal. https://www.verywellmind.com/five-stages-of-grief-4175361

Carney, K. (2020). Grief, Healing and the One-to-Two Year Myth. https://psychcentral.com/lib/grief-healing-and-the-one-to-two-year-myth/

Fahkry, T. (2017). Why Guilt and Shame Carry a Strong Burden: This Is How to Make Peace With Them and Transform Your Life. https://medium.com/the-mission/why-guilt-and-shame-carry-a-strong-burden-how-to-make-peace-with-them-and-transform-your-life-54ec6451fa2

Holland, K. (2018). What You Should Know About the Stages of Grief. https://www.healthline.com/health/stages-of-grief

James, A. (2020). How To Deal With Intense Sadness And Sorrow After A Death. https://www.betterhelp.com/advice/grief/how-to-deal-with-intense-sadness-and-sorrow-after-a-death/

Love Lives On. (n.d.). 5 Stages of Grief & How to Survive Them. https://www.loveliveson.com/5-stages-of-grief/

Moorhead, J. (2017). How to Live and Learn From Great Loss. https://www.theguardian.com/lifeandstyle/2017/mar/04/how-to-live-and-learn-from-great-loss-death

Mendoza, M.A. (2018). Five Common Myths About Grief. https://www.psychologytoday.com/us/blog/understanding-grief/201808/five-common-myths-about-grief

Royden, L. (2019). Numbed Out: When Feelings Freeze Up After a Bereavement. *https://www.psychologytoday.com/us/blog/the-mourning-after/201906/numbed-out-when-feelings-freeze-after-bereavement*

Rumi Quotes. (n.d.). BrainyQuote.com. *https://www.brainyquote.com/quotes/rumi_597890*

Shermer, M. (2008). Five Fallacies of Grief: Debunking Psychological Stages. *https://www.scientificamerican.com/article/five-fallacies-of-grief/*

Smith, M., Robinson, L. & Segal, J. (2019). Coping With Grief and Loss. *https://www.helpguide.org/articles/grief/coping-with-grief-and-loss.htm*

What's Your Grief. (2019). Feeling Nothing During Grief: The Experience of Emotional Numbness. *https://whatsyourgrief.com/feeling-nothing-during-grief/*

Wolfelt, A.D. (2018). Grieving VS. Mourning. *https://www.taps.org/articles/24-3/grieving-vs-mourning*

Printed in Great Britain
by Amazon